SECRET BRADFORD

MARK DAVIS

AMBERLEY

First published 2014

Amberley Publishing
The Hill, Stroud
Gloucestershire, GL5 4EP

www.amberley-books.com

ISBN 978 1 4456 4359 5 (print)
ISBN 978 1 4456 4394 6 (ebook)

British Library Cataloguing in
Publication Data.
A catalogue record for this book is
available from the British Library.

Typesetting by Amberley Publishing.
Printed in the UK.

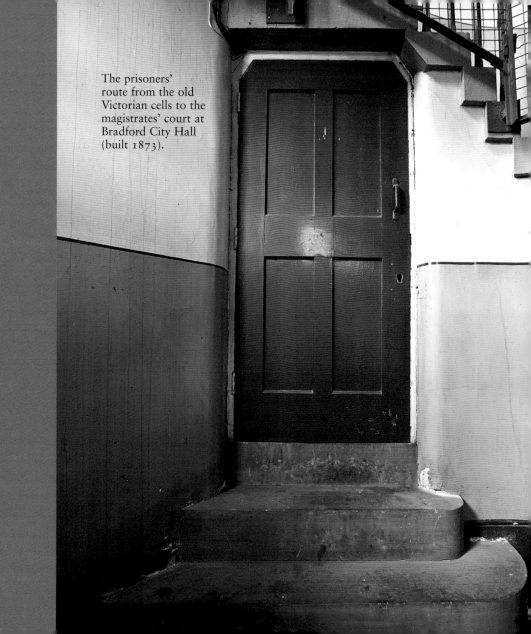

The prisoners' route from the old Victorian cells to the magistrates' court at Bradford City Hall (built 1873).

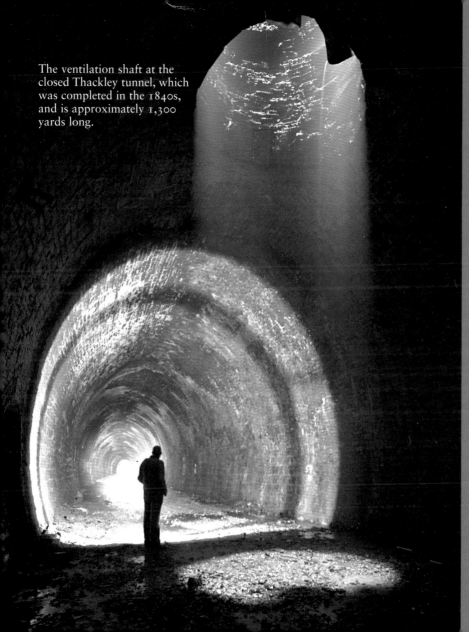

The ventilation shaft at the closed Thackley tunnel, which was completed in the 1840s, and is approximately 1,300 yards long.

CONTENTS

ACKNOWLEDGEMENTS

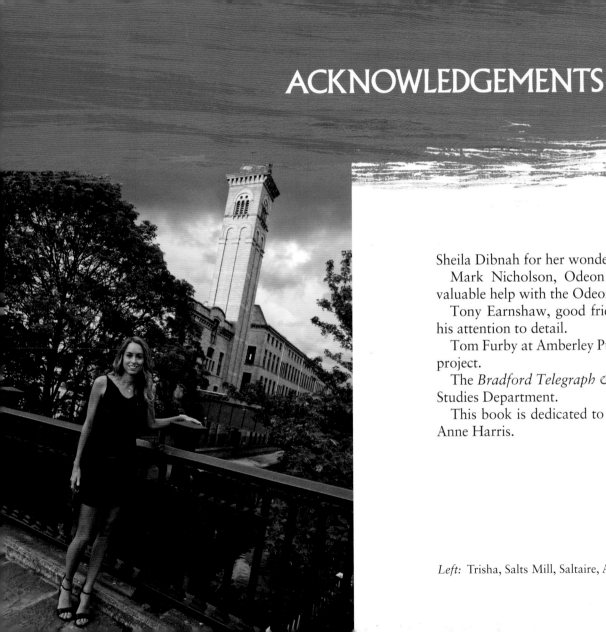

Sheila Dibnah for her wonderful, thought-provoking foreword.

Mark Nicholson, Odeon Historian and Campaigner for his valuable help with the Odeon history.

Tony Earnshaw, good friend, colleague and fellow author for his attention to detail.

Tom Furby at Amberley Publishing for all his hard work on this project.

The *Bradford Telegraph & Argus* and Bradford Libraries Local Studies Department.

This book is dedicated to my partner, the beautiful Trisha Jill-Anne Harris.

Left: Trisha, Salts Mill, Saltaire, August 2014.

FOREWORD

My late husband Dr Fred Dibnah MBE was famous for felling industrial chimneys. A keen historian, he was surprisingly sensitive when it came to matters of architecture. He'd labour intensely for a week preparing for the death-knell of one of these fine nineteenth-century structures. As the pit props burned away, weakening the smokestack, I once asked, 'Why not just blow it up with dynamite?' He pulled a stern face and replied, 'Dignity love, these things deserve dignity. Some bloke spent time making it beautiful and it mattered back then that things were created with pride.'

I realised why Mark approached me to write this foreword. Yes, perhaps my famous last name is part of it, but certainly not all. And it doesn't matter what side of the Pennines you are from when it comes to appreciating the past; if you love it, it's there – wherever you live. As a kid I would rummage amongst the detritus of old factories and climb into derelict buildings taking delight in seeing something others were missing. I'd find an old piano in a house, a heavy safe in a shop with no roof; chairs and beds in abandoned places. The peeling paint, pipes and relics, left as they were, untouched and returning to their natural state; the musty smell and sound of dripping water off in the distance; mould growing on discarded skips of cotton bobbins and reams of paper from some empty spinning mill, strewn about the floor, left and no longer important. The dark shadows and rusty shapes in an old abandoned plastic works (before it later became a carpet warehouse).

These two talented men, experts in their own fields, have a lot in common; Fred spoke passionately on film about the past, and Mark brings it alive through the lens of a camera. The end result is the same: the rich tapestry of a bygone era is captured, ensuring we see the faded, terrible beauty in decaying things … in those secret, abandoned places, with their echoes and ghosts of the past, once created with dignity and pride. Some preserved, some lost forever.

Sheila Dibnah

INTRODUCTION

Finally reaching double figures, this book being my tenth publication with Amberley Publishing, it seems fitting that I focus on the very city I was born in. As a child, one of my favourite pastimes was exploring old buildings; in particular the old Baird Television works near Artic Parade off of Great Horton Road. The building was full of oscilloscopes and various electrical equipment on what seemed like hundreds of work benches stretching as far as the eye could see. How I wish I had taken pictures now. Interestingly, Artic Parade, I was to learn later, was the very road my grandmother, as a young girl, would walk down in all weathers in her clogs on the cobbles to her place of work at Cannon Mills.

Bradford, as we know, is famous for its worsted cloth industry, which is reflected in this book by the various mills included. In addition, I have tried to balance the contents with other locations, such as cinemas, churches and even a mortuary chapel. When choosing the title it was difficult to choose between 'hidden' or 'secret' Bradford. In the end I decided to go with secret Bradford in the sense that many of the locations will be new to the reader, while others have been photographed from angles previously unseen.

The reality is that this book is full of ghosts. Many of the images were taken in the previous four years, and of buildings that are no longer there or have been altered. Certainly, as time passes, and given the fragile nature of change, the majority of the locations will disappear. The reader will note the common theme that runs through the pages. Bradford is incredibly unlucky with regards to fires destroying the workplaces, and leisure facilities of our fathers and grandfathers. Fire, as we know, when unchecked takes no prisoners; hence many of the places affected were demolished immediately after, rendering grade II listing of no value. My intention with this book was to create a lasting record of locations important at a time when industry and manufacturing was king. Just as I research locations from Victorian and Edwardian photographs now, I would like to think my work here will be a point of reference in another century in the future.

Although potentially depressing to see our heritage being swallowed by fire and demolition, there is without a doubt a beacon of light beginning to illuminate Bradford again. After years of stagnating, great things are beginning to happen, and with that comes major investment. In 2014, Bradford represents a multicultural society on the up. If you thought Bradford was over, then think again. If you are in any doubt ask my friend Gary Peacock, the manager of the Midland Hotel, which is more than likely to go through a success not previously seen since the boom years of the industrial revolution, thanks to the building of the new Broadway shopping centre close by. For me, the image is everything, and I have gone to incredible lengths to bring something different to the reader including climbing 300 feet cranes.

Mark Davis,
August 2014

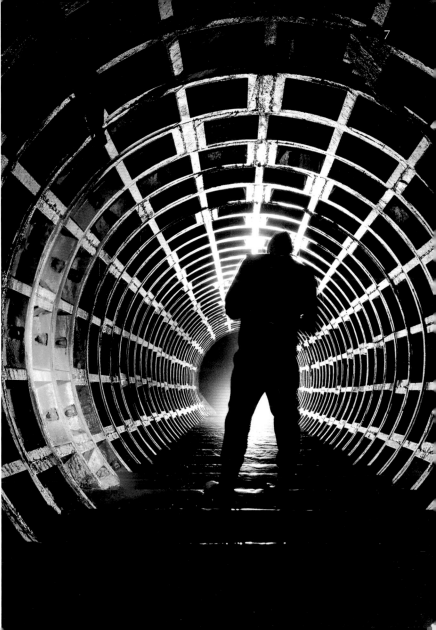

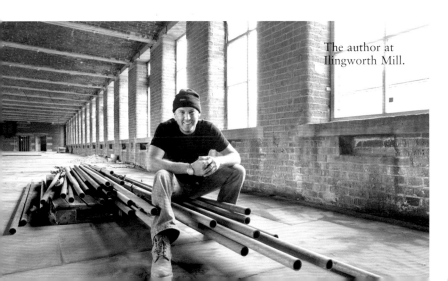

The author at
Ilingworth Mill.

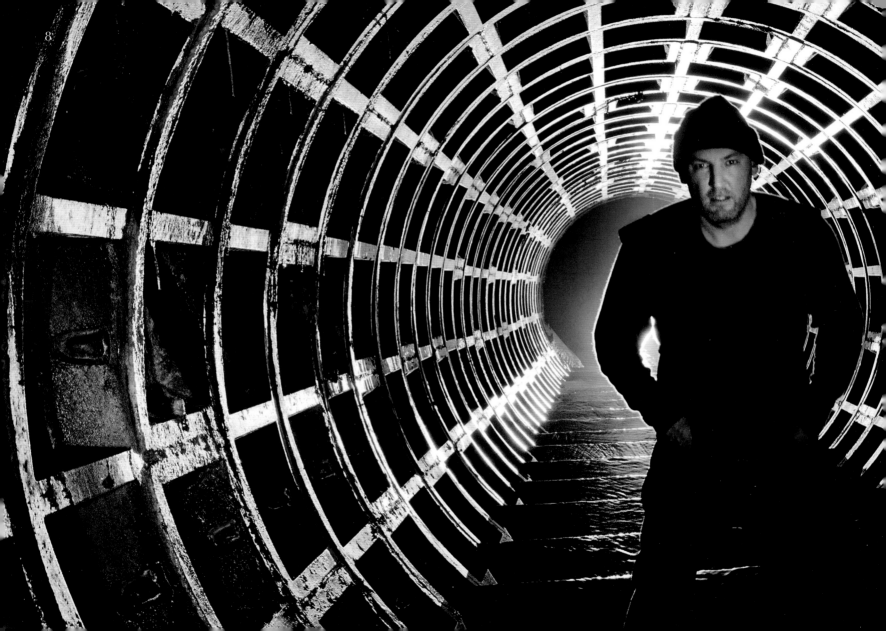

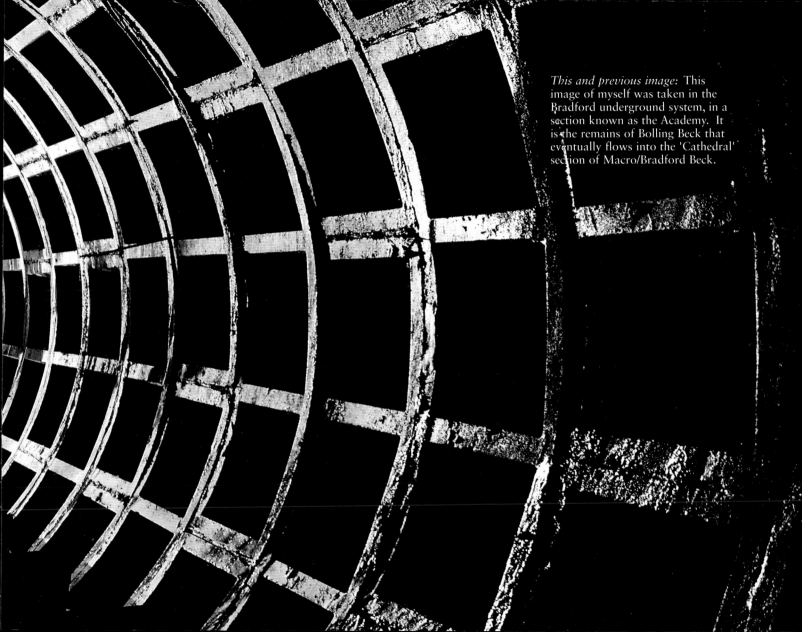

This and previous image: This image of myself was taken in the Bradford underground system, in a section known as the Academy. It is the remains of Bolling Beck that eventually flows into the 'Cathedral' section of Macro/Bradford Beck.

DALTON MILLS, KEIGHLEY

Although not in located in Bradford, this particular mill has a BD postcode and is certainly worthy of inclusion. Dalton Mills was once the largest textile mill in the region, employing more than 2,000 workers. It was built by Joseph Craven in 1869 and replaced the original mill, which was owned by Rachel Leach in the 1780s. The mill was named after a man called Dalton, the manager employed by Rachel Leach.

In its heyday, between 1869 and 1877, the mill provided jobs for workers all over Keighley and the Worth Valley. As the textile industry declined the fortunes of Dalton Mills changed and, up until 2004, it had been virtually empty for almost a decade. John Craven, the great-great-grandson of Joseph, who had built the mill, eventually chose to sell Dalton Mills to ensure its survival. Part of the renovation of the clock tower has included restarting the impressive clock, which has not ticked for twenty-five years. In the mill's prime, thousands of workers relied on the clock to get to work on time, but the hands had not moved for a quarter of a century. The clock has since been repaired, so it can display the time to the whole

of Dalton Lane again. The partially restored mill, which had a starring role as Marlborough Mills in the BBC adaptation of North and South, suffered a devastating fire in January 2011. The blaze, which wrecked a derelict wing of the mill, was confirmed as being the result of an arson attack by West Yorkshire Fire & Rescue Service.

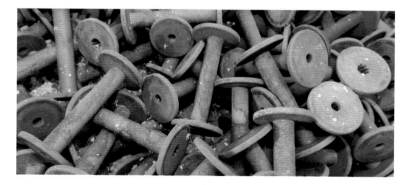

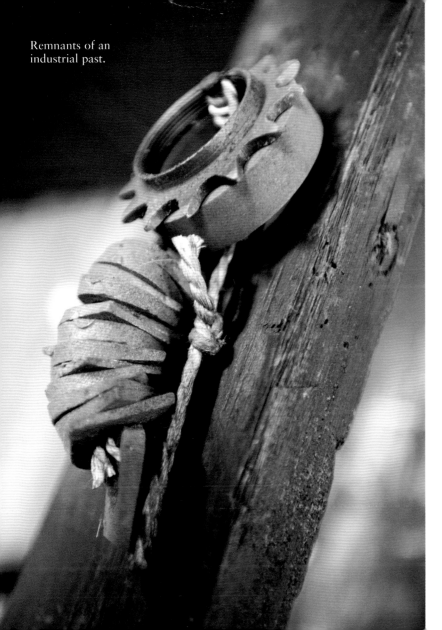

Remnants of an industrial past.

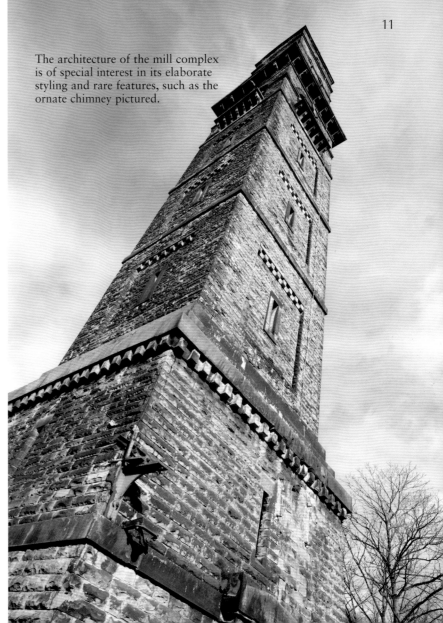

The architecture of the mill complex is of special interest in its elaborate styling and rare features, such as the ornate chimney pictured.

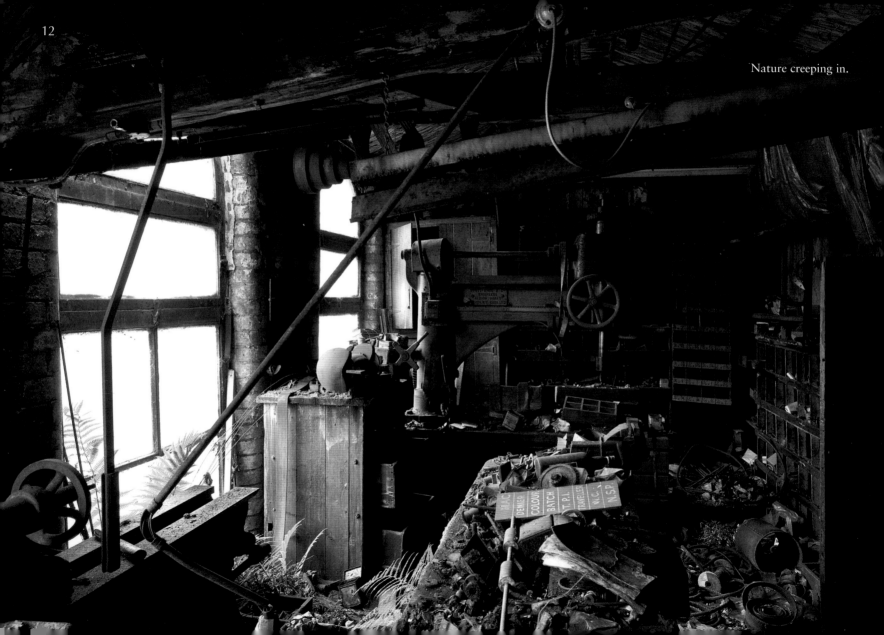

Nature creeping in.

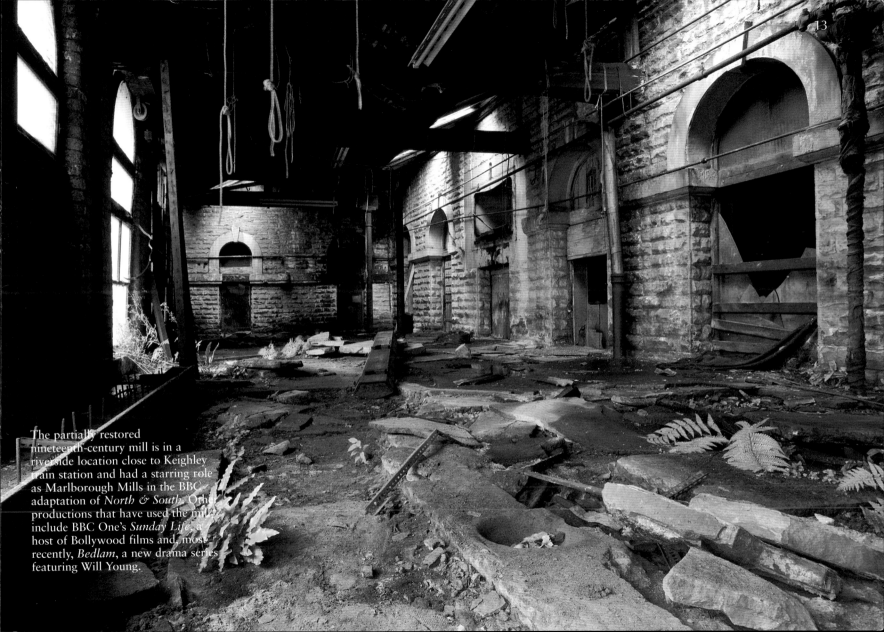

The partially restored nineteenth-century mill is in a riverside location close to Keighley train station and had a starring role as Marlborough Mills in the BBC adaptation of *North & South*. Other productions that have used the mill include BBC One's *Sunday Life*, a host of Bollywood films and, most recently, *Bedlam*, a new drama series featuring Will Young.

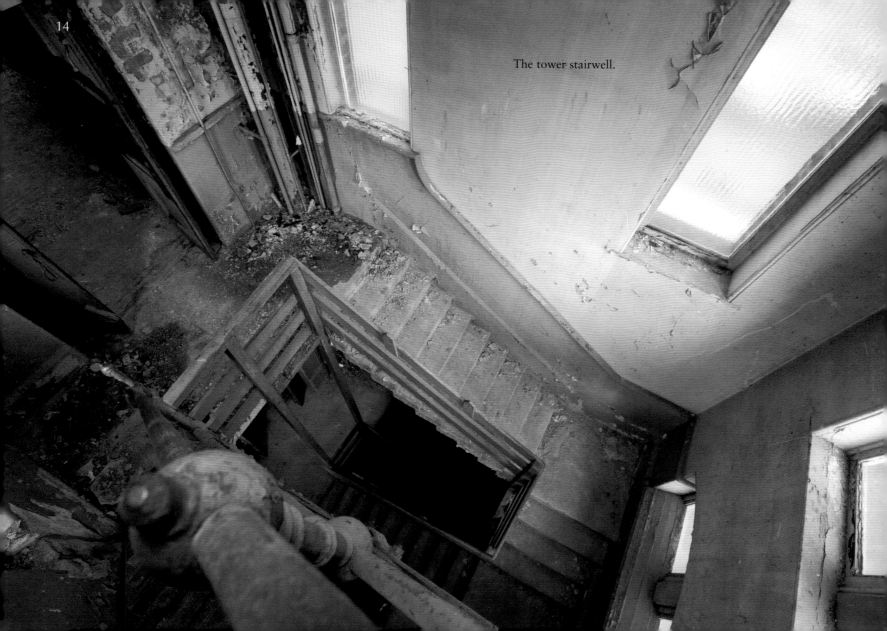

The tower stairwell.

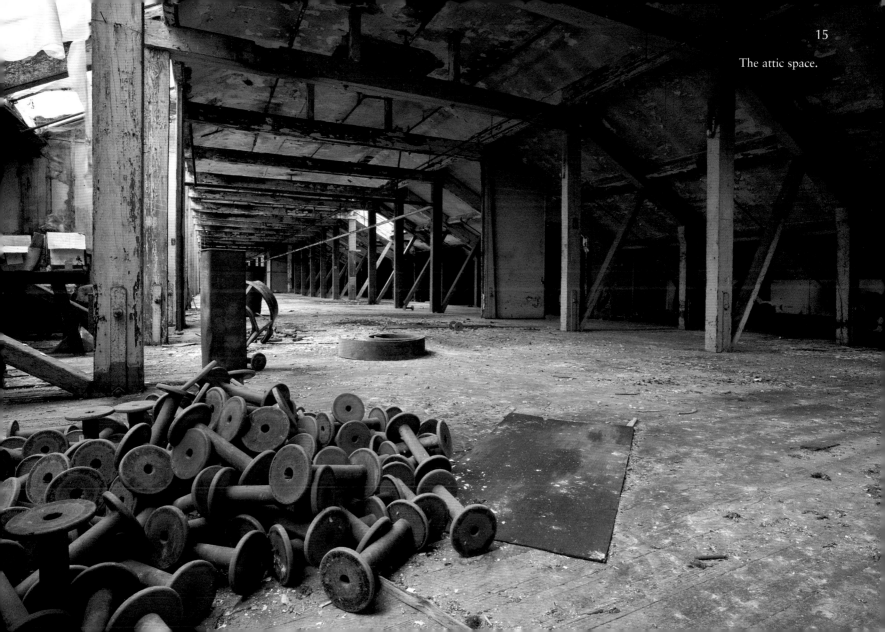

The attic space.

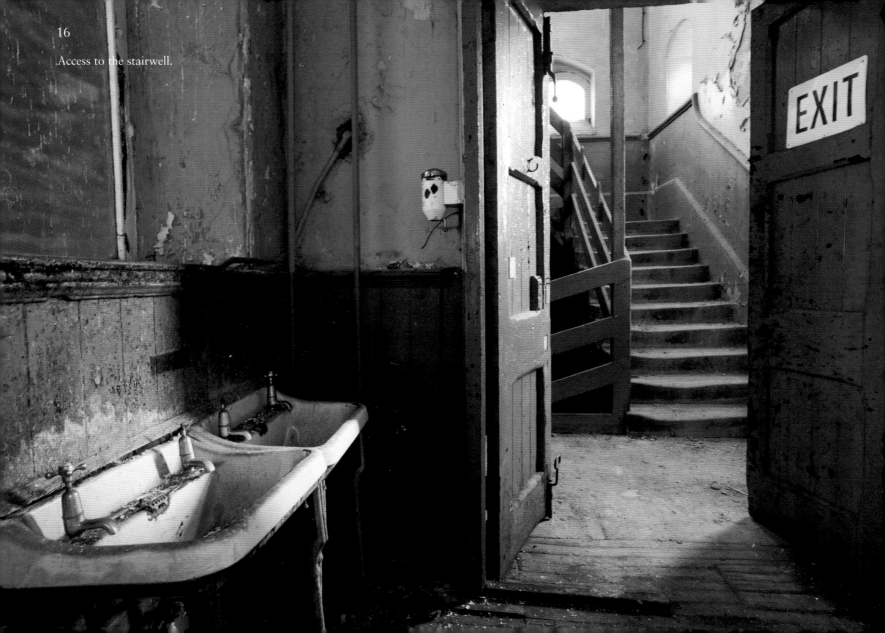

Access to the stairwell.

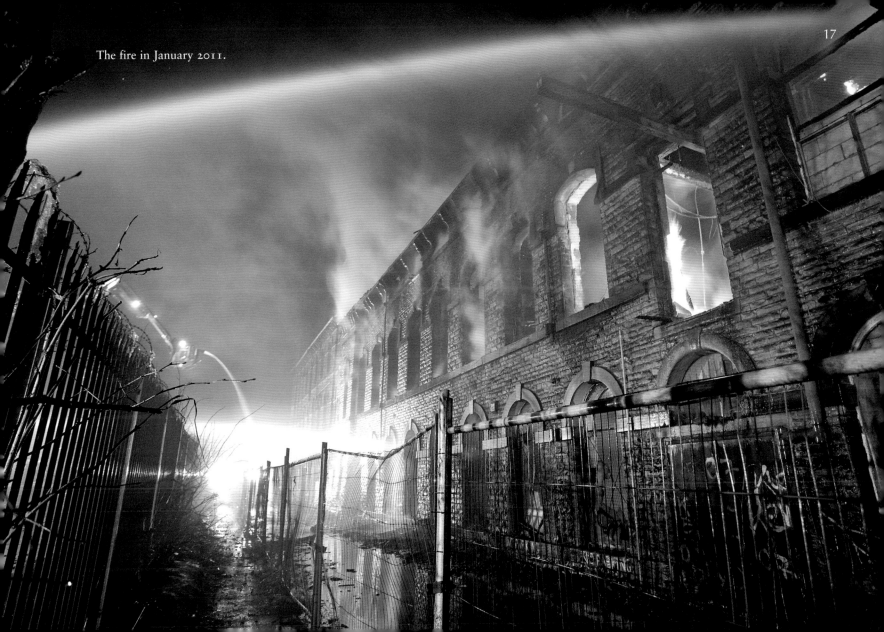

The fire in January 2011.

My image that appeared in the
Telegraph & Argus, 2011.

Telegraph & Argus

telegraphandargus.co.uk

Monday, January 3, 2011   45p   Serving the district for 141 year

TODAY IN BRIEF

Driver arrested after boy dies

A man has been arrested on suspicion of drink-driving and causing the death of a teenage pedestrian after revellers watched in horror as the 16-year-old boy was hurled over a 6ft steel fence after a collision outside an Otley church. ≫ Page 2

174 city homes plan revived

A mothballed plan to build 174 homes on the site of a former hospital in Odsal, Bradford, is being revived by the project's developers. ≫ Page 7

£5,000 premium shock for driver

Motorists in Bradford are still being hit with high insurance premiums with one driver quoted more than £5,000. ≫ Page 11

Residents urged to recycle more

Householders in Bradford are being asked to give the planet a belated Christmas present by recycling more. ≫ Page 13

WEATHER - Page 19

DAY: Cloudy and cold again   3C

NIGHT: Cold and some snow   0C

FLAMES: Firefighters direct jets of water at the raging blaze at Dalton Mills, Keighley, which is being treated as suspicious by investigators   Picture by Mark Da

ARSON PROBE AS BLAZE WRECKS HISTORIC MILL

Inferno at landmark building is treated as suspicious after 100 firefighters quell flames

A massive blaze which destroyed part of historic former textile mill is being treated suspicious, investigators have revealed.

About 100 firefighters from across the country worked through the night to tackle flames which poured from the empty Grade-II listed landmark building Dalton Mills, in Dalton Lane, Keighley.

Full story – P3

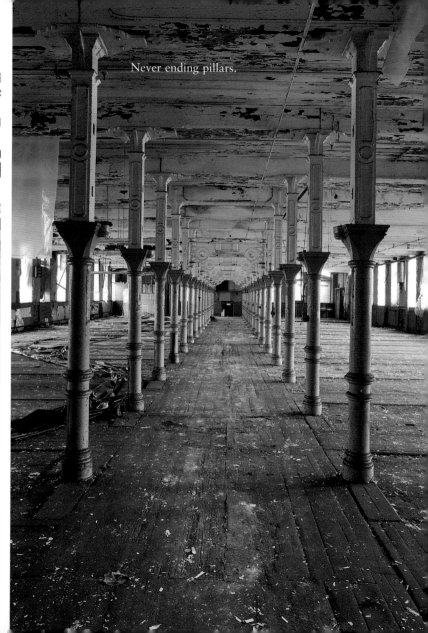

Never ending pillars.

DENHOLME VELVETS

In February 2009, it was revealed that one of Bradford's best-known textile firms had set out an extreme survival plan that involved demolishing the original mill buildings to make way for a housing development. This would enable funding, allowing them to focus their operations in a smaller unit. Denholme Velvets, which has operated in Halifax Road, Denholme, since 1938, hoped to secure the remaining fifteen jobs at the company by getting planning permission for its proposals. At its peak, Denholme Velvets was an internationally renowned velvet manufacturer employing about 150 people. The company was famous for its high-quality chiffon velvet, as well as specialised velvets for jewellery displays and other technical uses. Manufacturing had come to an abrupt halt about twelve months prior, in 2008, after the loss of the crucial market for making velvet for leading photographic companies during the digital revolution. Julian Armitage, managing director, at that time said, 'The demise of the photographic market was the final nail in the coffin for our manufacturing business. It was a really important market for us, and we supplied all the leading companies. We are hoping to get planning permission to redevelop the site, as we no longer need the large mill premises that were designed for 150 people.'

As part of the redevelopment plans, the land to the east of the Halifax Road site was to be leased to Denholme Clough Cricket Club free of charge, to allow it to continue playing on the site. In 2014, the site of the old building is a wasteland after demolition took place approximately two years ago.

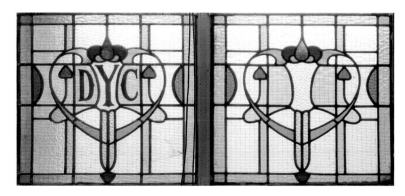

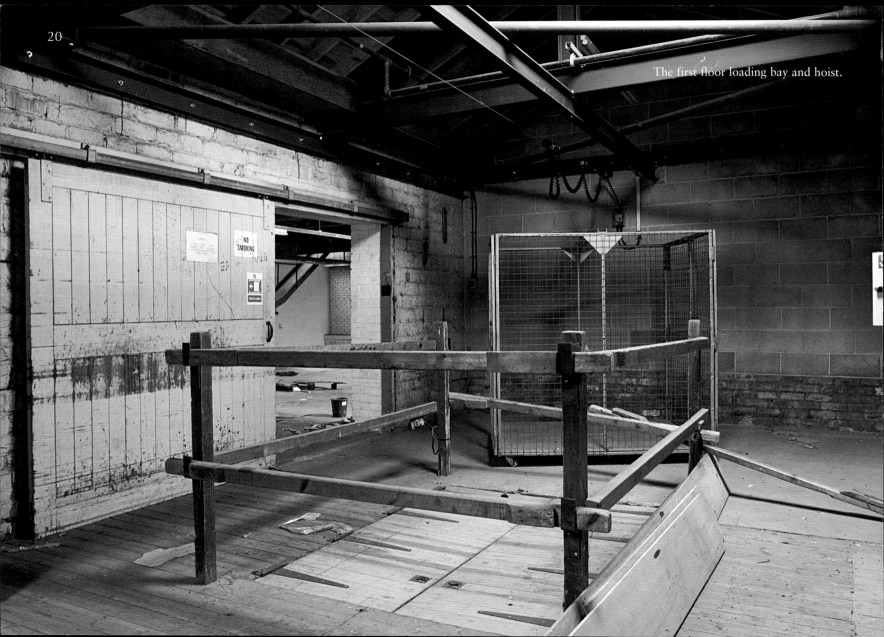

The first floor loading bay and hoist.

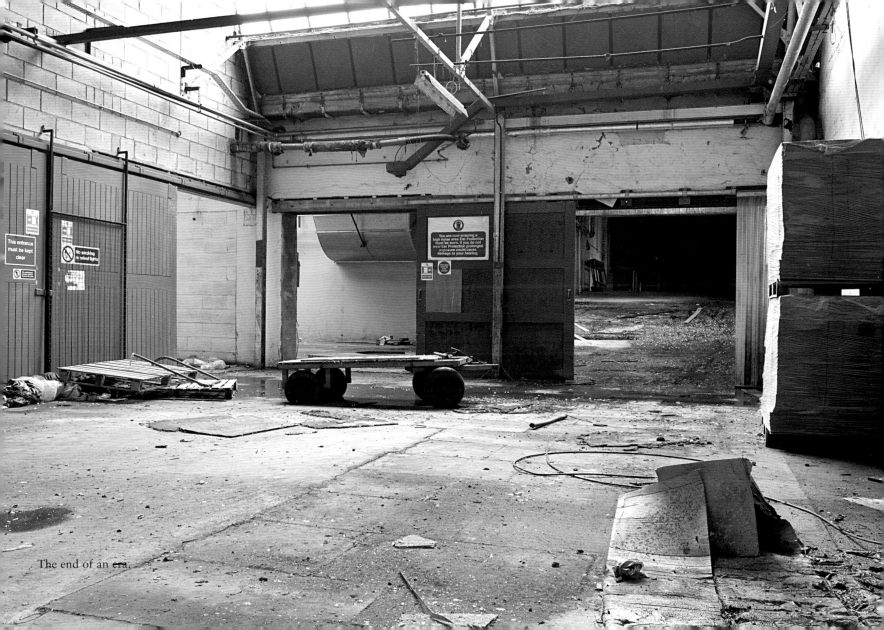

The end of an era.

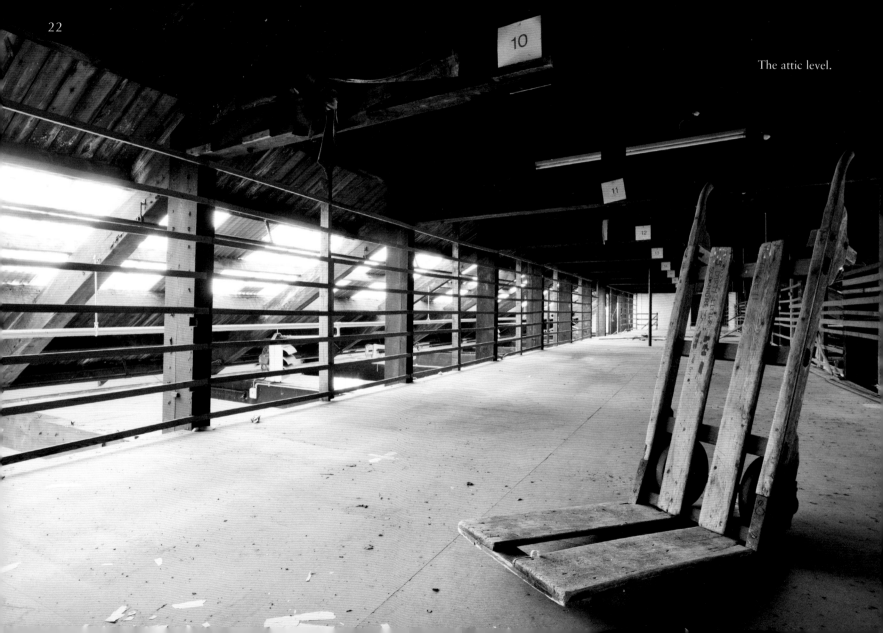

10

The attic level.

The company was famous for its high-quality chiffon velvet.

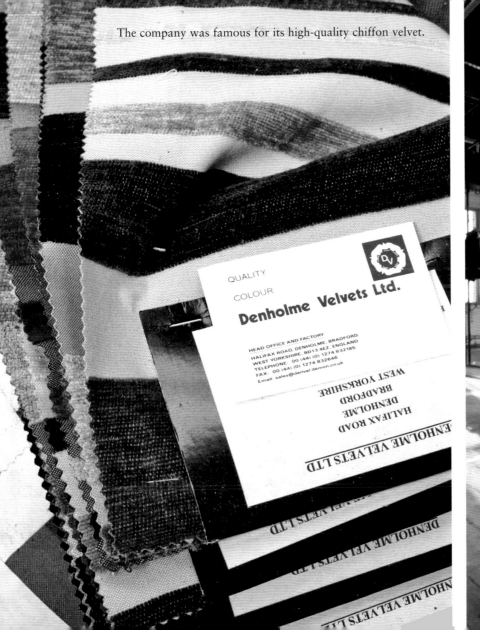

QUALITY

COLOUR

Denholme Velvets Ltd.

HEAD OFFICE AND FACTORY
HALIFAX ROAD, DENHOLME, BRADFORD,
WEST YORKSHIRE, BD13 4EZ, ENGLAND
TELEPHONE: 00 (44) (0) 1274 832185
FAX: 00 (44) (0) 1274 832646
Email: sales@denvel.demon.co.uk

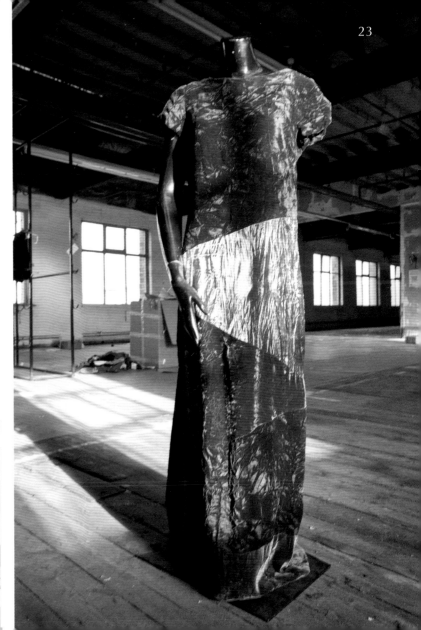

GLENROYAL CINEMA

Beginning life as the Shipley Picture House Company, this later became the Glenroyal Cinema Company. The building sited adjacent to the Leeds–Liverpool Canal was designed by the Manchester architect Ernest Dawson. The foundation stone was laid in March 1932 by Councillor Clifford Cawthorne, the retiring chairman of Shipley Urban District Council and a director of the new cinema company. The opening ceremony on Monday 5 September 1932, was by Councillor Gordon Waddilove JP, the incoming chairman of Shipley Urban District Council, followed by the film Emma, starring Marie Dresler, Richard Cromwell and Myrna Loy, plus 'a laughable comedy', together with a live jazz band performance and a soloist.

For sixty years or more the Glenroyal building was an important functioning feature of central Shipley. The cinema when built was a building of singularly beautiful design yet eminently practical... The front elevation was of rustic brick and cream terracotta faience tiling, which was illuminated with floodlights. The entrance hall had gold plastic walls and a mother-of-pearl dome ceiling; beautiful Spanish mahogany doors that gave a hint of the beauty to follow within. The wide central stairway led directly to the balcony foyer magnificently carpeted with thick Wilton carpet, specially woven by Firth's of Brighouse for the Glenroyal and supplied and fitted by Alfred Linley & Sons of Windhill. The illuminated red and black Buddha statue on the staircase was bought at an auction by the owner, Shack Hyde, who found it attractive and adopted it as a mascot. It seems that more Buddhas appeared at other cinemas in his expanding circuit – some were on public display and others were in offices. From the balcony, which seated 350, one realised the immensity and beauty of the building and a decorative scheme of green and gold to 'give an impression of space and life which will enable the mind of the patron to relax into a world of pleasurable imagination'.

As this was 1932 and 'talkies' were now well established, the Glenroyal was fitted with the American-designed Western Electric Sound System. The decision to install this system followed a lengthy investigation in which the directors visited more than sixty cinemas to hear various makes of talkie apparatus under working conditions before making their final commitment. In 1953, a 'new wide dimension screen' was installed and the seating capacity reduced slightly by removing some front-row seats due to the large screen size. Certainly this was the very first installation of the new generation of wide curved screens in the Bradford/Shipley area and probably in Yorkshire. The Glenroyal was the first cinema in the area (after the Ritz in Bradford) to show 3-Dimensional films – the latest craze from the USA with images appearing to jump out at you.

The Glenroyal closed as a cinema on 8 December 1962. Since then it has been converted into firstly a casino and then a bingo hall. Information gathered from the memoirs of the late Colin Sutton, Bradford cinema historian.

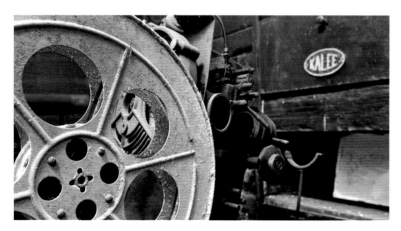

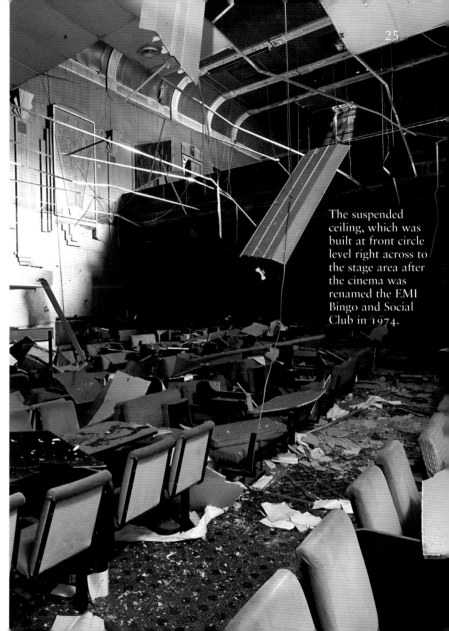

The suspended ceiling, which was built at front circle level right across to the stage area after the cinema was renamed the EMI Bingo and Social Club in 1974.

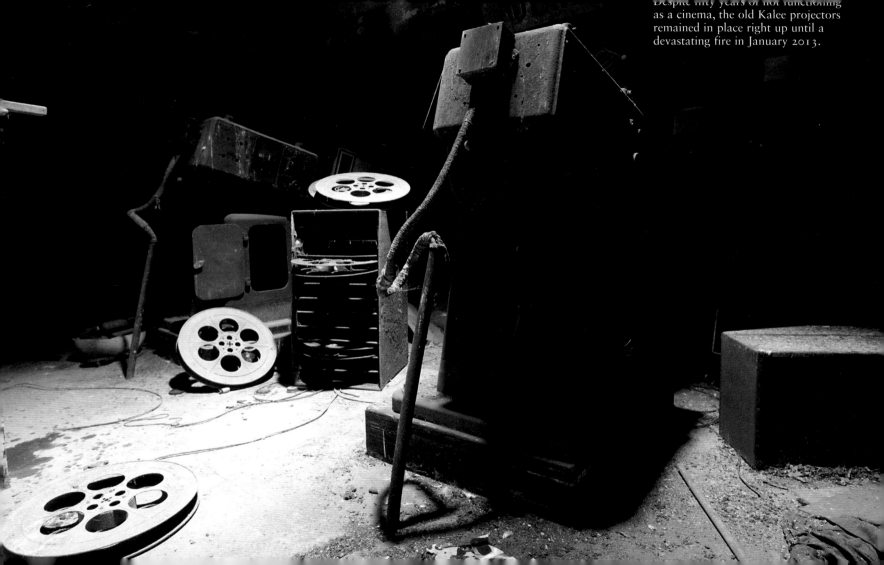

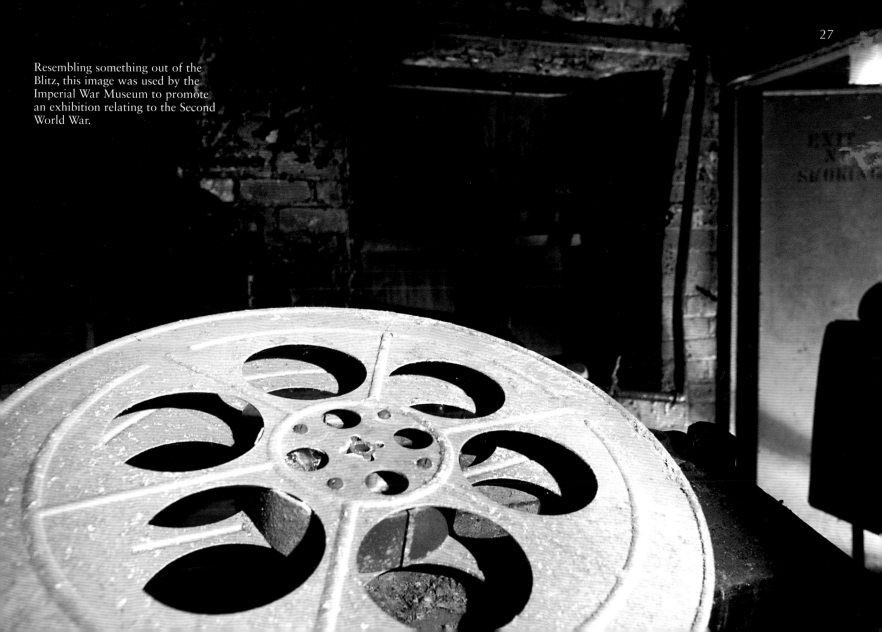

Resembling something out of the
Blitz, this image was used by the
Imperial War Museum to promote
an exhibition relating to the Second
World War.

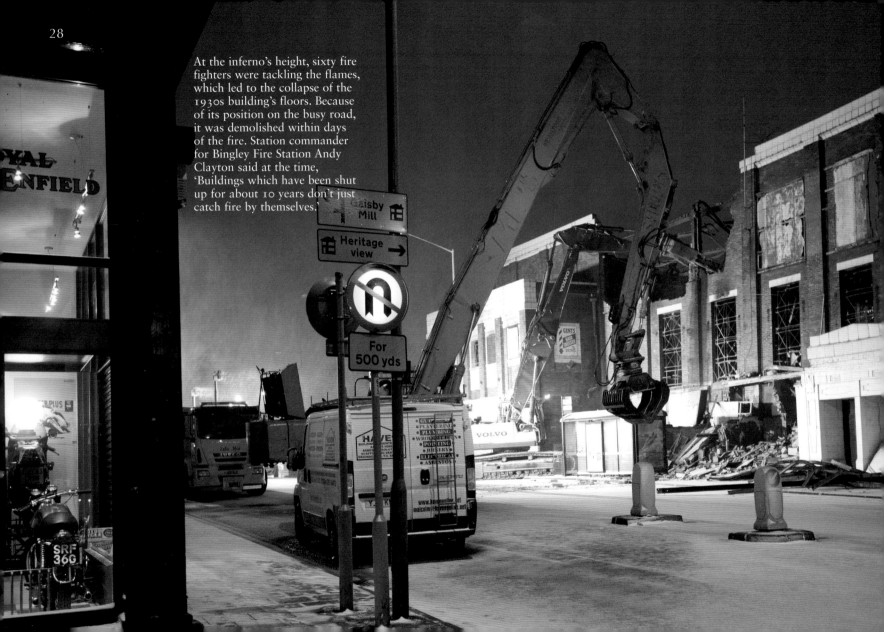

At the inferno's height, sixty fire fighters were tackling the flames, which led to the collapse of the 1930s building's floors. Because of its position on the busy road, it was demolished within days of the fire. Station commander for Bingley Fire Station Andy Clayton said at the time, 'Buildings which have been shut up for about 10 years don't just catch fire by themselves.'

BRICK LANE MILLS, H. HEY & CO. LTD

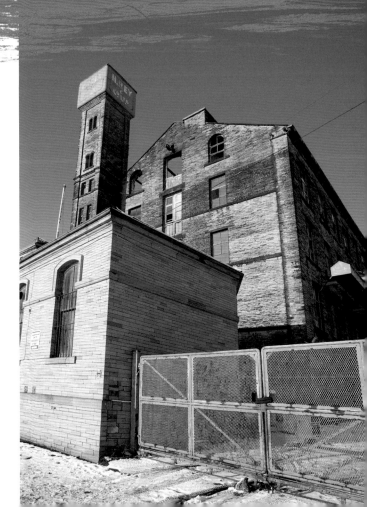

Although Brick Lane Mills were purpose built around 1894 for Alfred Priestman & Co., it is clear that, in 1879, Alfred was already operating on the site as a worsted spinner, the address being 240a Thornton Road. Later, in 1903, the vast complex was stated to be located at 242 Thornton Road where Alfred was in business as a fancy worsted woollen manufacturer. Business must have been good for Alfred to allow such expansion. Certainly he was well connected and attended with other important Bradford men various important functions and ceremonies including the lavish funeral of Charles Semon, the former mayor of Bradford.

By 1953, the mill was in the hands of H. Hey & Co. Ltd, Worsted Spinners, who incidentally were in business in Keighley as early as 1903. Little else is known about the mills with the exception that a fire broke out in June 2007. For many years, the complex stood out on Thornton Road because of its blue tower with white painted lettering H. Hey & Co. Ltd. The fire that devastated the mill put paid to any hope of salvaging the build, and in the summer of this very year the bulldozers moved in and completed the demolition.

Despite in a derelict state the old
buildings retained some of their
dignity and were still impressive prior
to demolition.

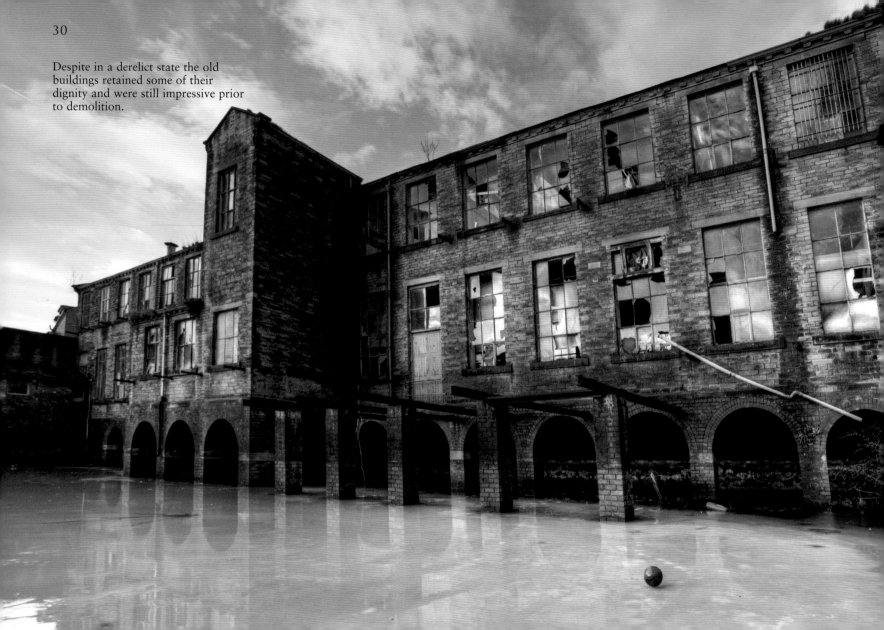

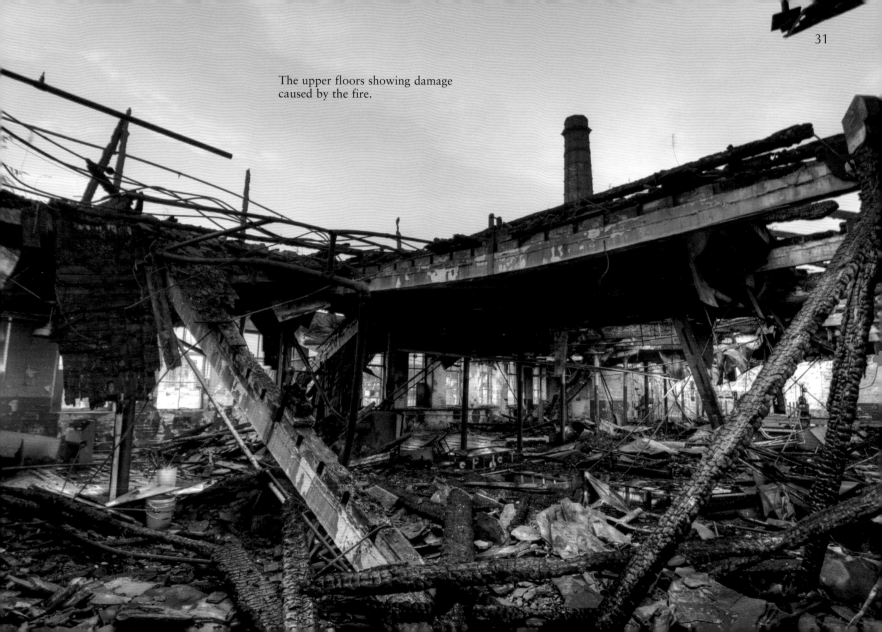

The upper floors showing damage caused by the fire.

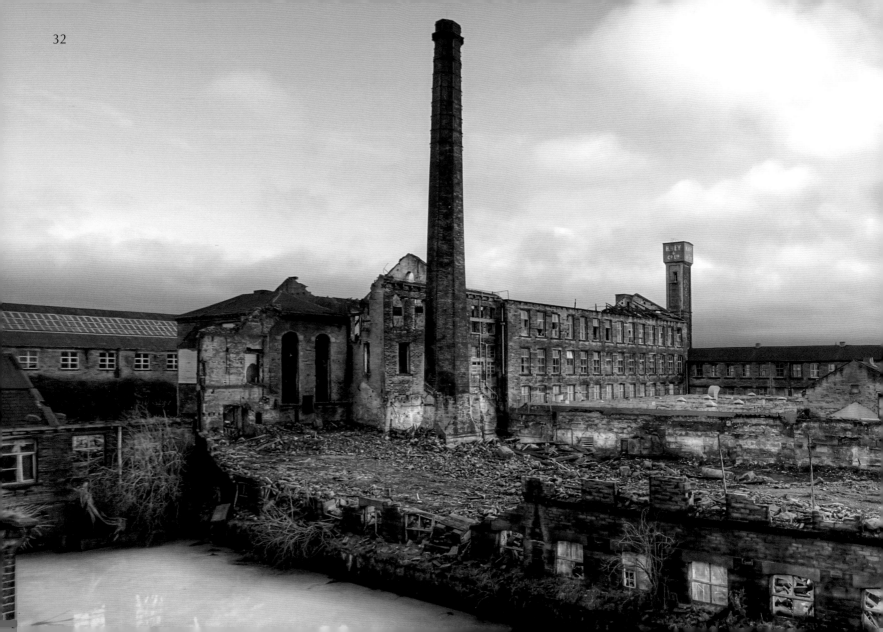

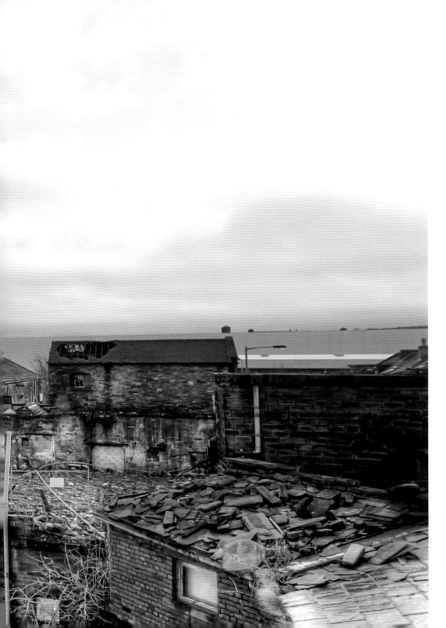

Resembling a scene from the Blitz, the skeleton of the old engine shed can be seen to the immediate left of the mill chimney. The site was totally cleared in the summer of 2014 when all the existing buildings were demolished.

QUEENSBURY GNR RAILWAY TUNNEL

Queensbury Tunnel was built by the Great Northern Railway between the years 1874–78. At 2,001 yards long, it is one of the longest and deepest railway tunnels in England. During its working life it serviced the Northern industrial towns of Bradford, Halifax, and Keighley. The passenger train service, however, ceased nearly sixty years ago in 1955. By all accounts one of the biggest problems in the tunnel's history was the formation of giant icicles on winter nights. In order to combat the problem, a steam engine would be parked there overnight in later years. The line was known as the 'Alpine Route' due to its hilly nature.

Derelict for decades, the tunnel is in desperate need of repairs, for which the Highways Agency is ultimately responsible. It was reported by the BBC in February 2014 that the tunnel could be converted into Europe's longest cycle path if campaigners get their way. The fear is that the owners may just fill it in with concrete to save money on the expensive repairs required. By utilising the tunnel for cycles, it would enable cyclists to avoid steep, traffic-clogged roads and provide a direct link between Bradford and Halifax.

Graffiti left by previous visitors
indicating the working years.

Queensbury Tunnel has not been used
by trains for almost 60 years and is
flooded in parts.

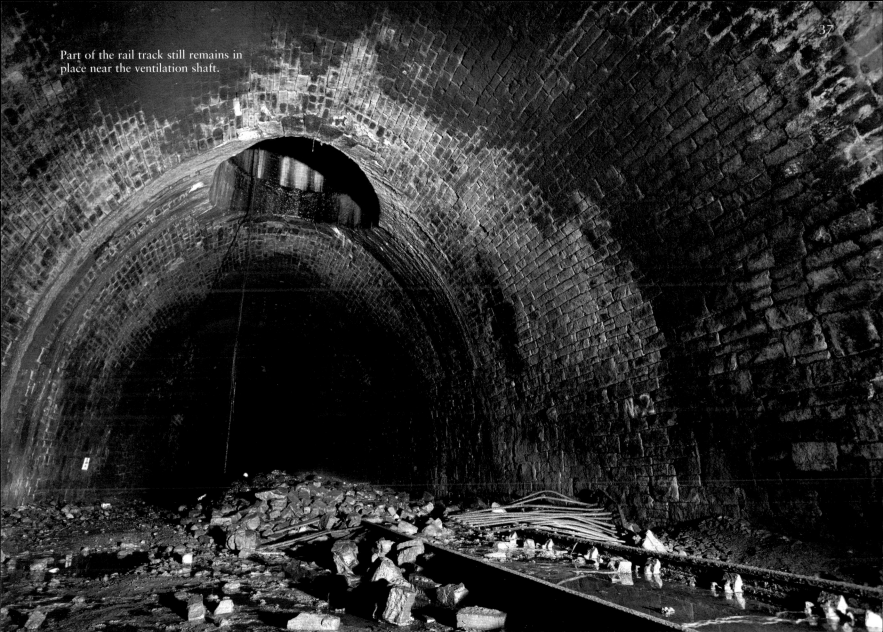

Part of the rail track still remains in place near the ventilation shaft.

THE ODEON

Built to the architectural specifications of Alderman William Illingworth, the former Bradford Odeon cinema first opened its doors in September 1930 as the New Victoria. This sumptuous palace of entertainment was capable of entertaining a house capacity of 3,318 patrons with a film, stage show (complete with an in-house orchestra) and a Wurlitzer Organ recital, all during the same programme. A ballroom and restaurant was housed in an adjoining wing. At the time of opening it was the third largest cinema in the UK.

The cinema became the Gaumont in September 1950, and in doing so it became the North's premier indoor concert venue. Many performances took place on the 70 foot wide stage during the next two decades, including pantomimes on ice, ballet and numerous rock 'n' roll shows. Visits by Buddy Holly and The Beatles to Bradford's Gaumont Theatre are now considered as legendary moments in the city's twentieth century history. Tom Jones gave the final concert there in October 1968, a month before the original theatre was internally redeveloped. The increasing availability of television since the late 1950s had gradually rendered huge cinemas into uneconomical white elephants.

The cavernous auditorium was subdivided into twin cinemas at balcony level and a bingo hall was inserted into the former stalls beneath. The building reopened as the Bradford Odeon and Top Rank Bingo during the latter part of 1969. Arguably, the most celebrated occasion of this era was the debut of the first *Star Wars* film in February 1978, which is remembered today for the long queues it commanded and the pre-titles spectacular mirror ball display.

As multiplex cinemas began to establish themselves as part of the UK's picture-going experience in the late 1980s, the Bradford Odeon responded to the local demand for a wider film choice by opening up the long-disused ballroom as an additional screen in June 1988.

Although a much-loved cinema steeped in history and nostalgia, the Bradford Odeon's days became numbered at the turn of the Millennium. The Odeon never stood a chance against the mighty modern multiplex! The bingo hall had already been closed for three years when the Odeon screened its final films in July 2000.

The more valuable fixtures and fittings were removed and transferred to the new Odeon Multiplex at Thornbury, which opened the following weekend. The old Odeon was boarded up, but it was not the end of the story. The site became the unwanted focus of a redevelopment opportunity, which would have necessitated its demolition. A relentless campaign was undertaken by the Bradford Odeon Rescue Group, which included their triumphant 'Hug The Odeon' event in the summer of 2007. A reported 1,000 locals joined hands around the perimeter of the entire building to show its support.

At the time of writing, the Bradford Odeon is facing what is hoped will be a brighter future with a proposal to reverse the 1969 subdivision work and reintroduce the massive auditorium space as a twenty-first-century concert venue.

Mark Nicholson, Odeon historian and campaigner

Right: William Illingworth's architectural masterstroke was the tower entrances, thus forging the unmistakable relationship between the Odeon and the neighbouring Alhambra.

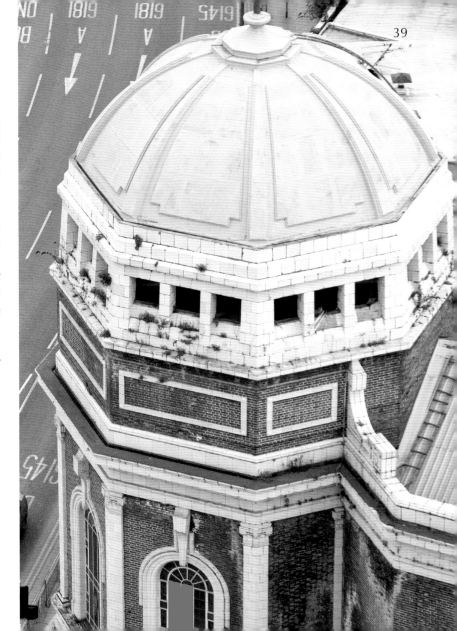

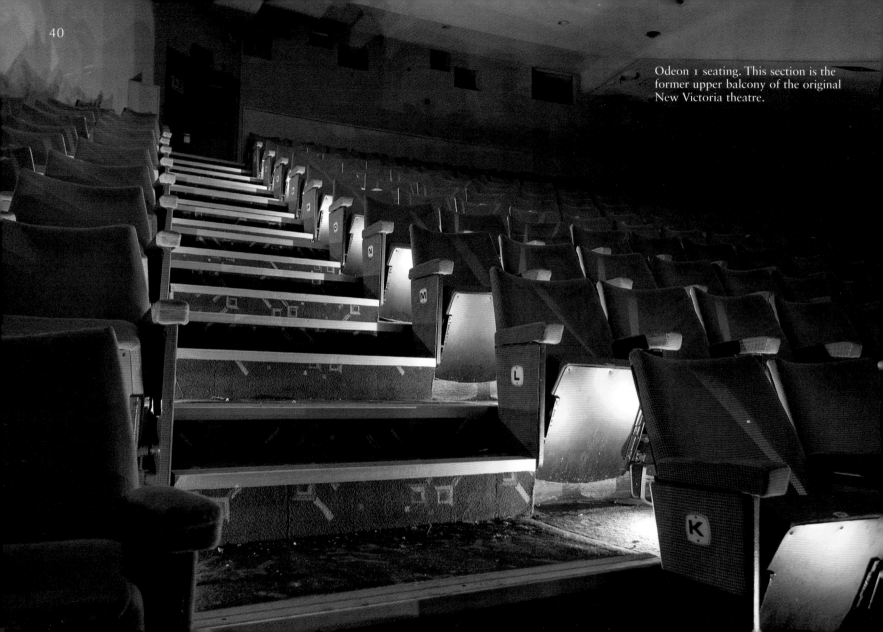

Odeon 1 seating. This section is the former upper balcony of the original New Victoria theatre.

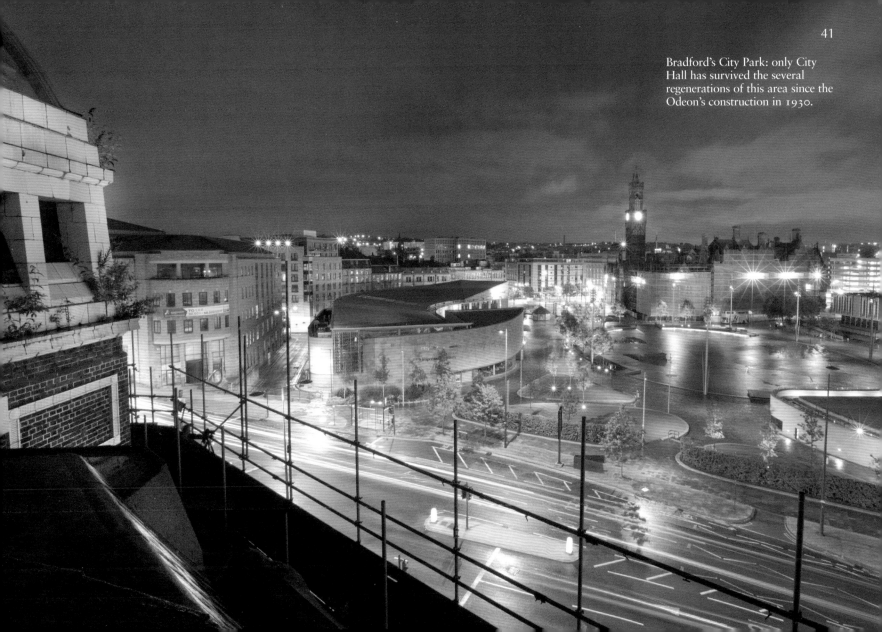

Bradford's City Park: only City Hall has survived the several regenerations of this area since the Odeon's construction in 1930.

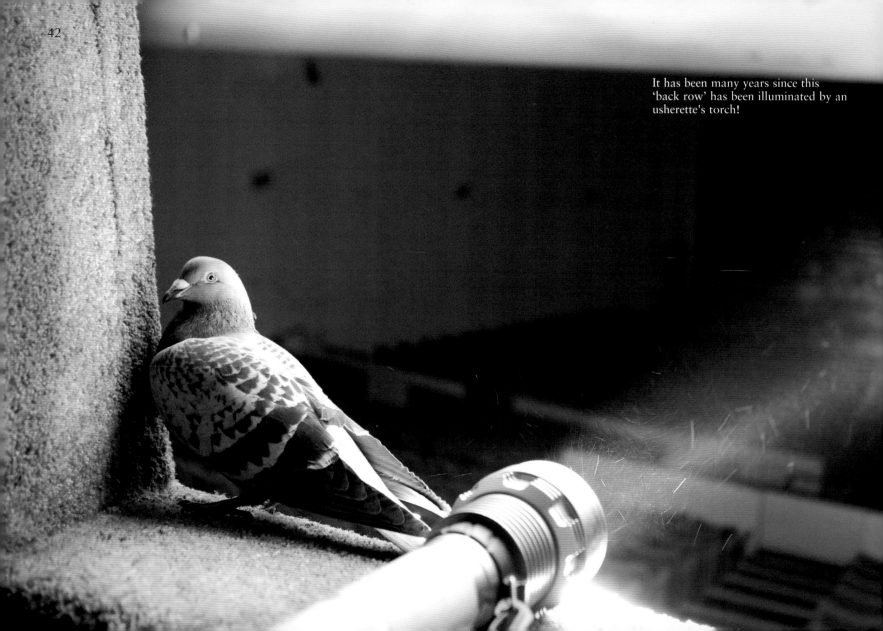

It has been many years since this 'back row' has been illuminated by an usherette's torch!

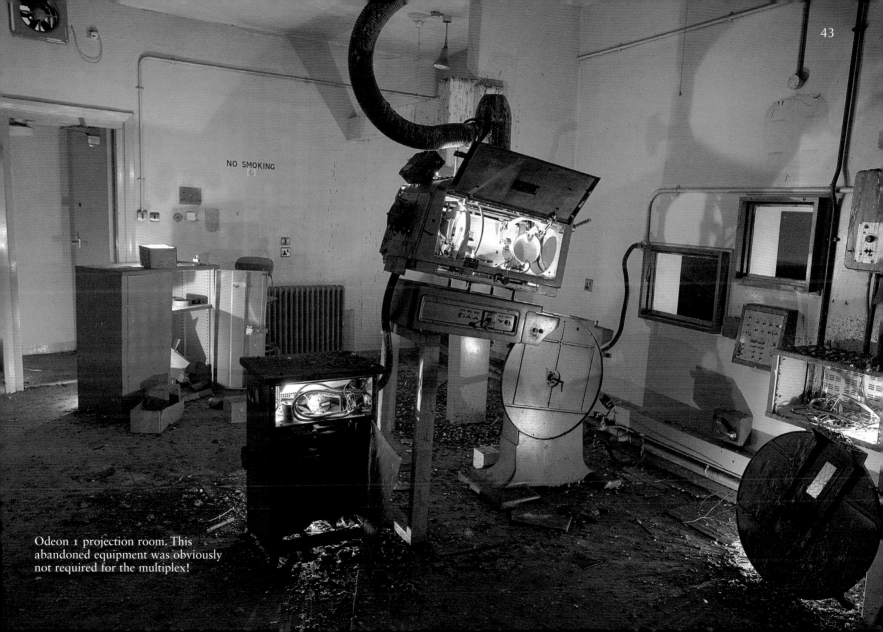

NO SMOKING

Odeon 1 projection room. This
abandoned equipment was obviously
not required for the multiplex!

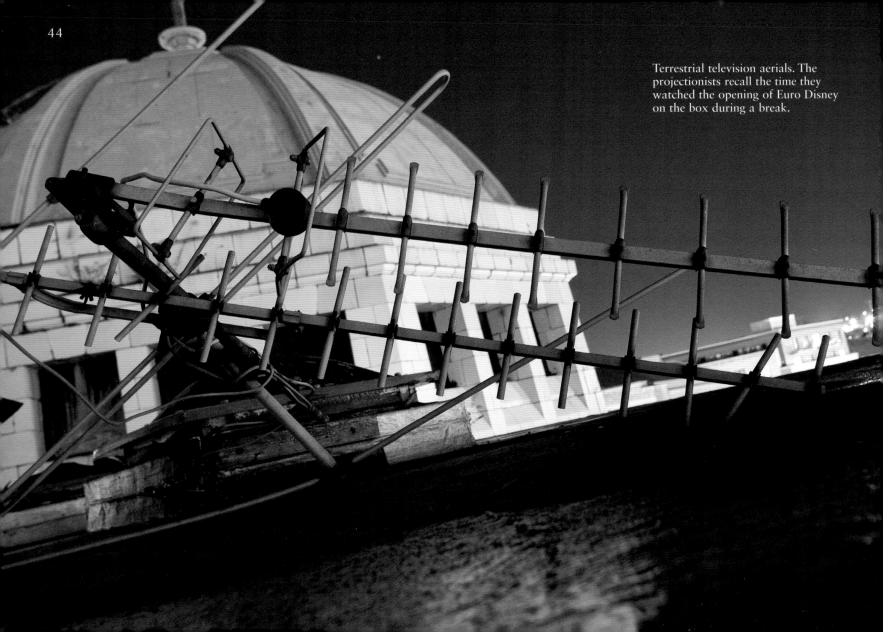

Terrestrial television aerials. The projectionists recall the time they watched the opening of Euro Disney on the box during a break.

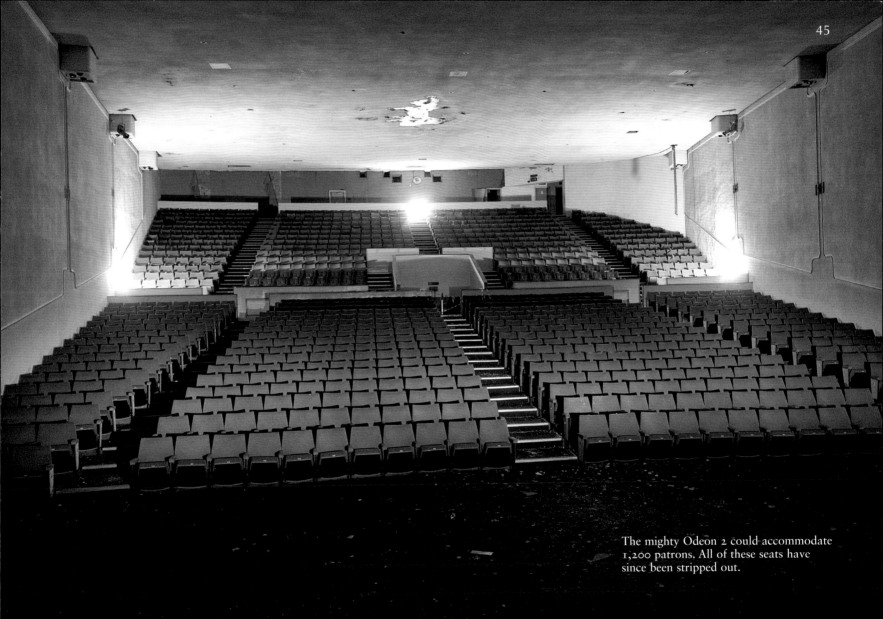

The mighty Odeon 2 could accommodate 1,200 patrons. All of these seats have since been stripped out.

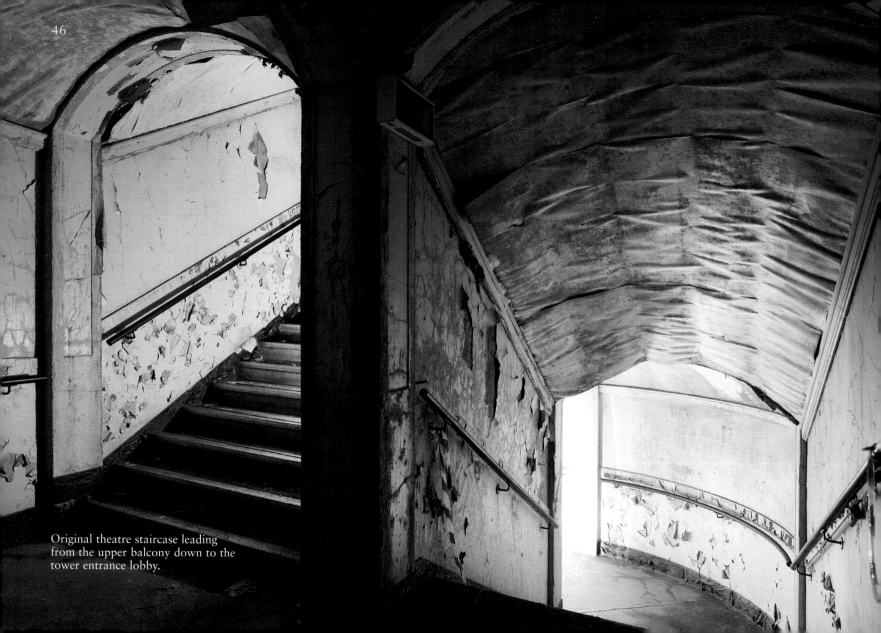

Original theatre staircase leading
from the upper balcony down to the
tower entrance lobby.

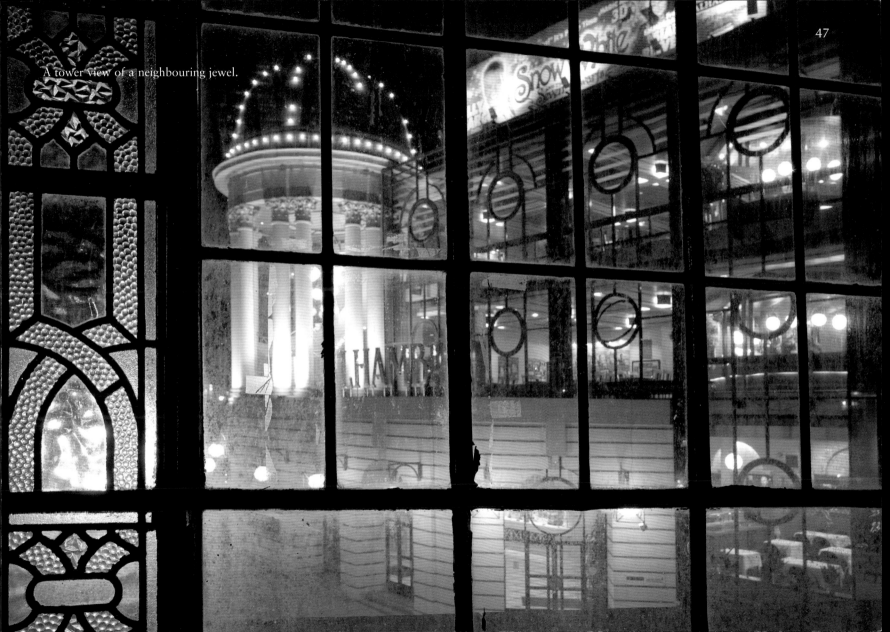

A tower view of a neighbouring jewel.

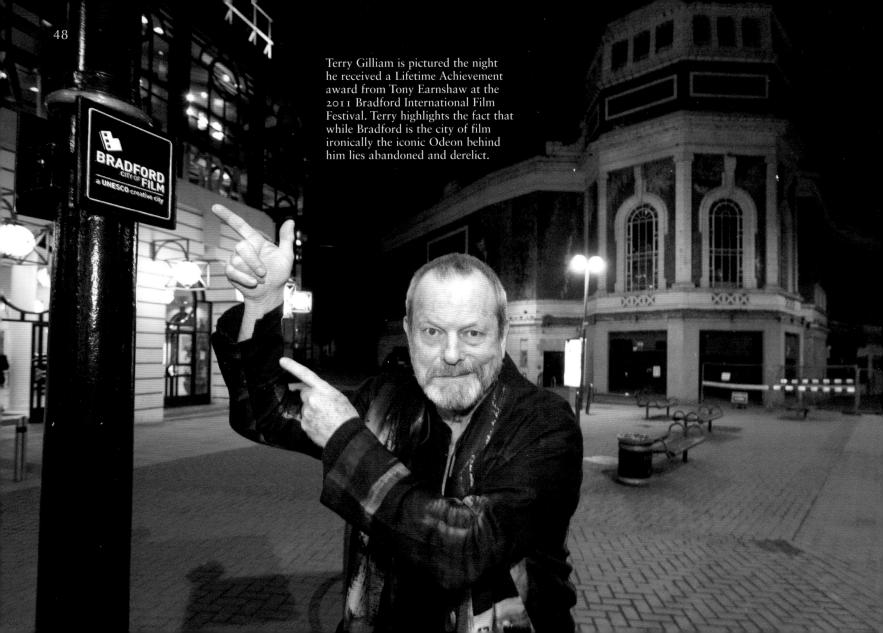

Terry Gilliam is pictured the night he received a Lifetime Achievement award from Tony Earnshaw at the 2011 Bradford International Film Festival. Terry highlights the fact that while Bradford is the city of film ironically the iconic Odeon behind him lies abandoned and derelict.

BRADFORD MECCA LOCARNO

When the Mecca Locarno opened in Manningham Lane in the early 1960s it was reputed to have cost over £500,000 to build. The now disused music and dance venue was built on the site of a former roller skating arena, which was burned to the ground in 1955. Over the years, this huge ballroom has changed hands many times. As a teenager I knew it as Dollars and Dimes, and my mother went there when it was the Mecca. In more modern times the venue was Maestros before being turned into Penningtons by Bradford businessman John Pennington, who sold it in 2003 when it became the Town & Country Club. In the past few years the venue has been the target of arsonists, yet to this day still remains; looking dishevelled, however, it is unlikely that it will ever operate as a nightclub again. The piece of land it stands on is within a council community priority area in the Unitary Development Plan. This means it needs to serve the local community as a community facility, housing for local needs or something that generates employment.

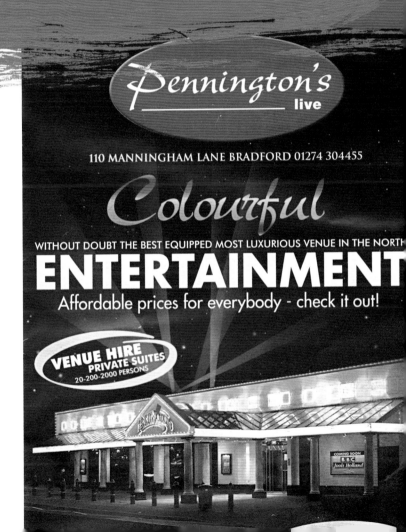

Externally, the old nightclub is a
shadow of its former self.

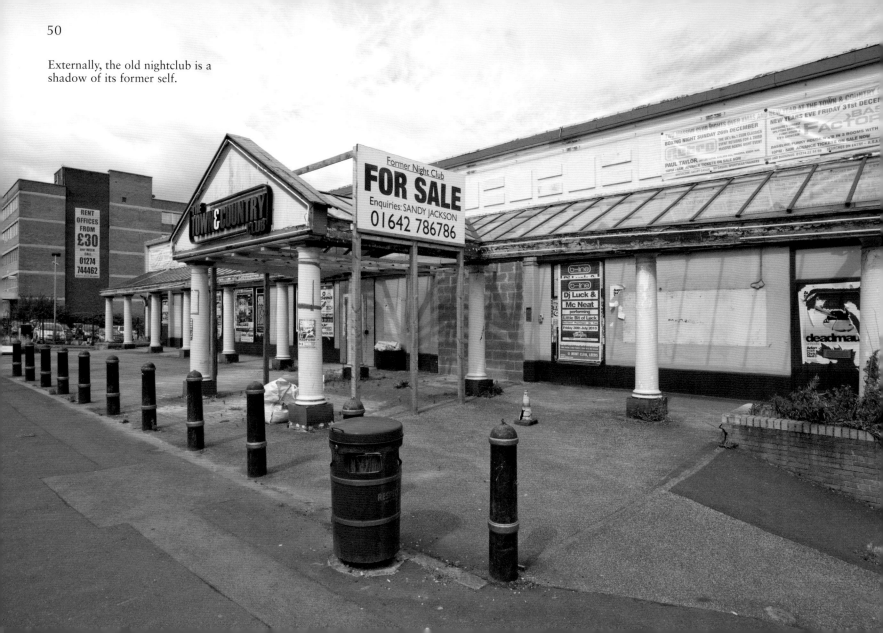

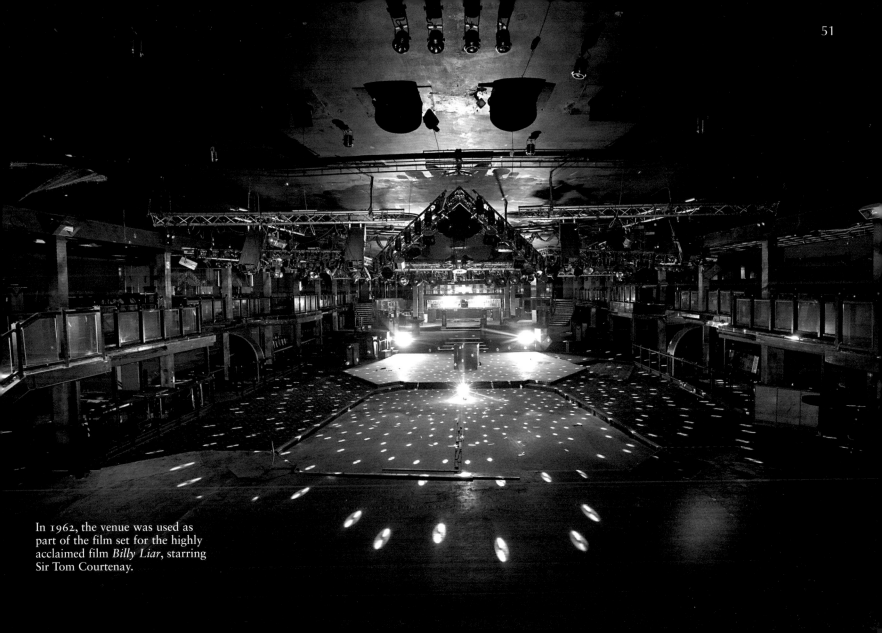

In 1962, the venue was used as part of the film set for the highly acclaimed film *Billy Liar*, starring Sir Tom Courtenay.

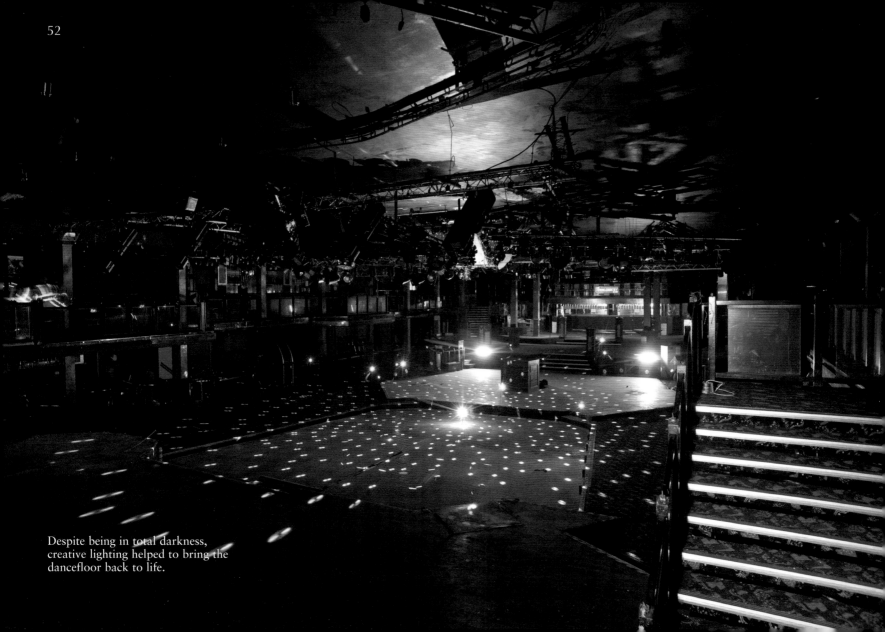

Despite being in total darkness,
creative lighting helped to bring the
dancefloor back to life.

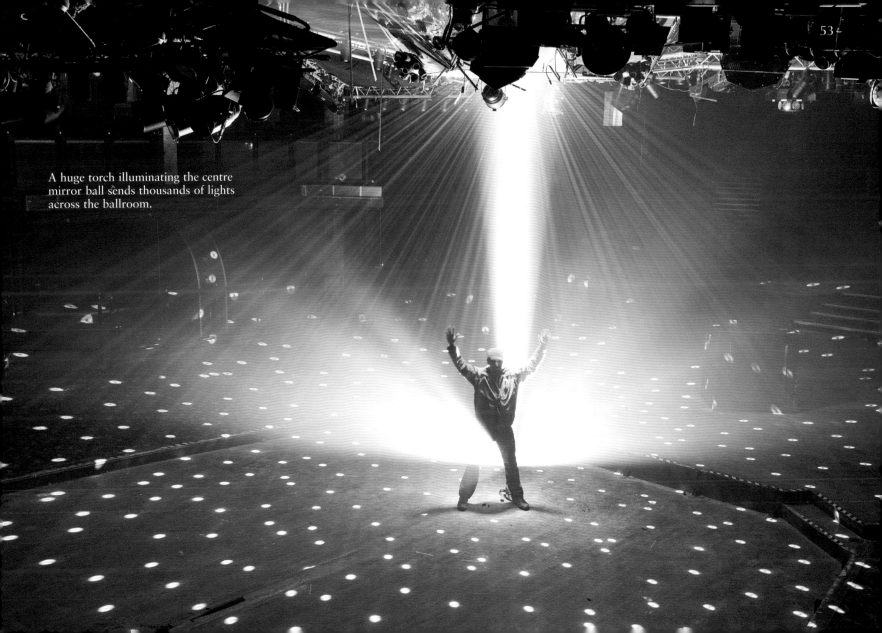

A huge torch illuminating the centre mirror ball sends thousands of lights across the ballroom.

CONDITIONING HOUSE, CAPE STREET

The Conditioning House, which is positioned opposite Midland Mills on Cape Street, was built by the Bradford Corporation. It followed a special Act of Parliament to quality check and control the moisture content of textiles by means of laboratory examination and certify their true weight and length. It was the only such one of its kind in this country. The purpose-built site was designed by F. Wild, who died in 1901 and sadly never saw his plans come to fruition. The work was instead supervised by city architect F. E. P Edwards. The structure was erected over four storeys, with a basement, around three sides of an open court. It opened in 1902.

Now, with its glory days a distant memory, the grade II listed building is starting to slip from the consciousness of the Bradford population and is increasingly neglected, forgotten and derelict. Since its closure in the late 1980s, it has struggled to find its way. In 1990, there were plans to transform the building into a hotel and conference centre. Six years later, permission was granted to convert it into commercial offices, but nothing happened. In the absence of attention, the building became ever more dilapidated. The Conditioning House is now privately owned and in 2010 Jim Dyson, director for owners Caddick, insisted his company was not about to throw in the towel on the project. Just like Midland Mills in 2014, Conditioning House still remains abandoned, awaiting investment.

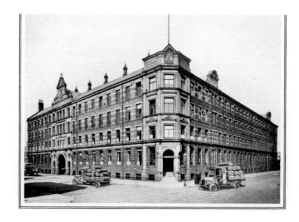

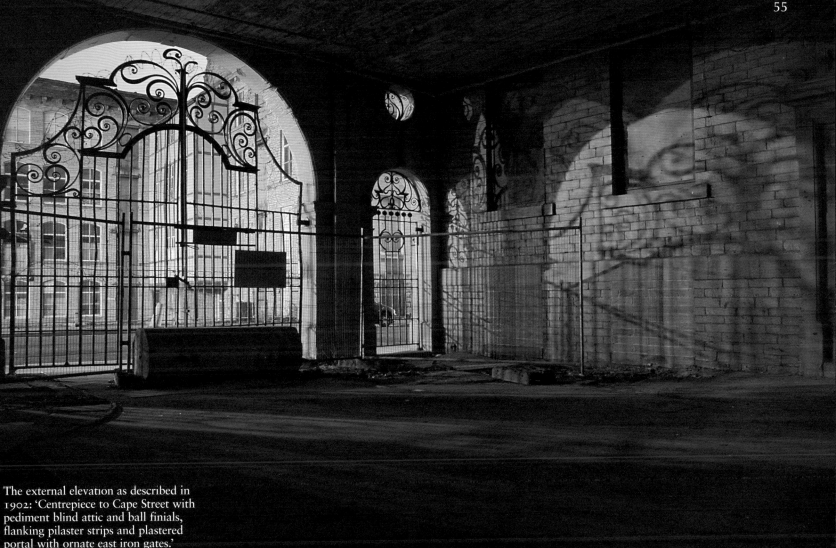

The external elevation as described in
1902: 'Centrepiece to Cape Street with
pediment blind attic and ball finials,
flanking pilaster strips and plastered
portal with ornate east iron gates.'

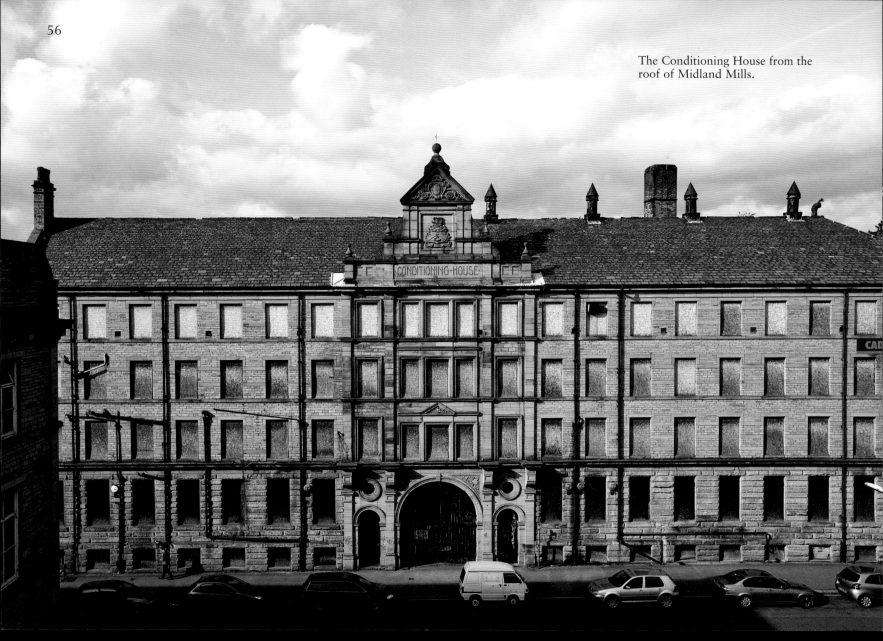

The Conditioning House from the roof of Midland Mills.

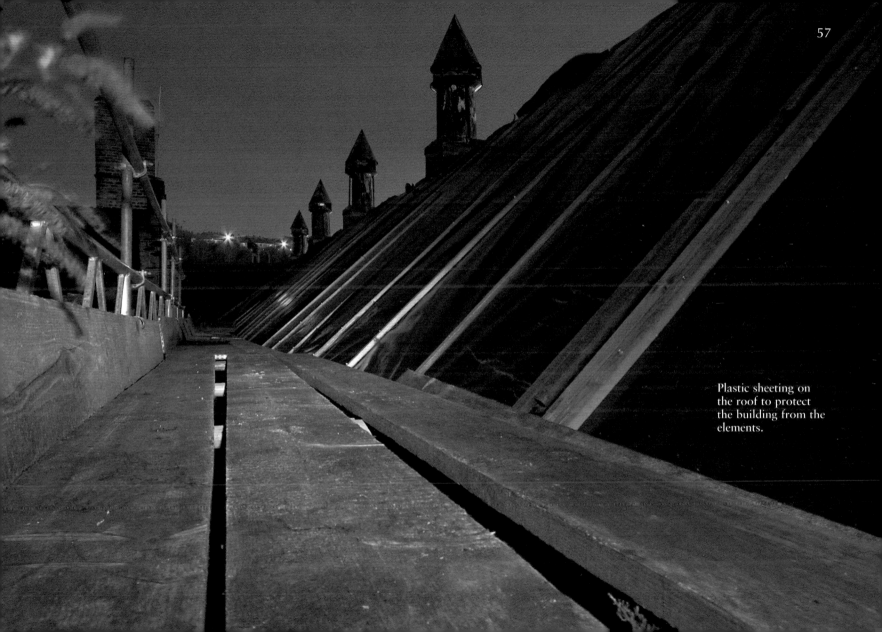

Plastic sheeting on the roof to protect the building from the elements.

The certificate office.

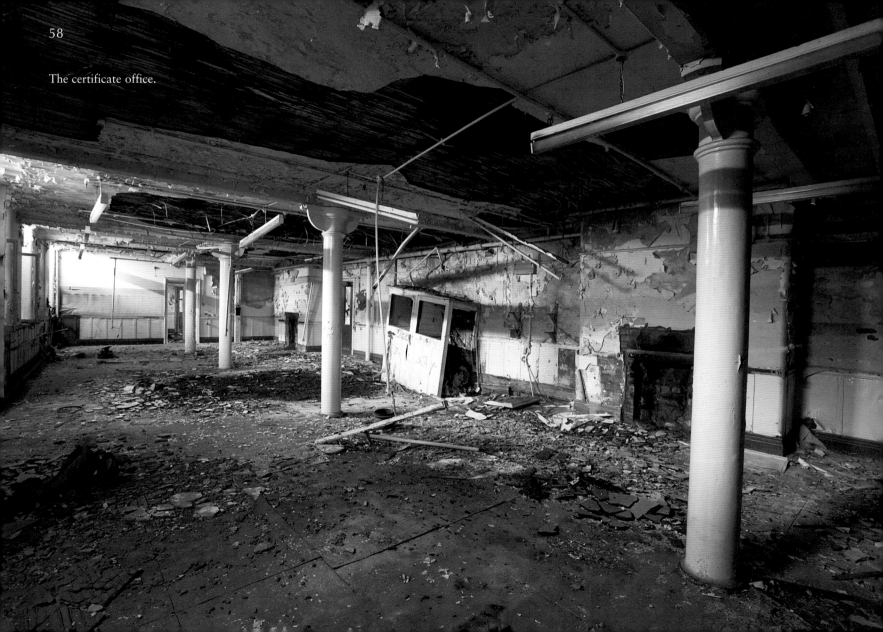

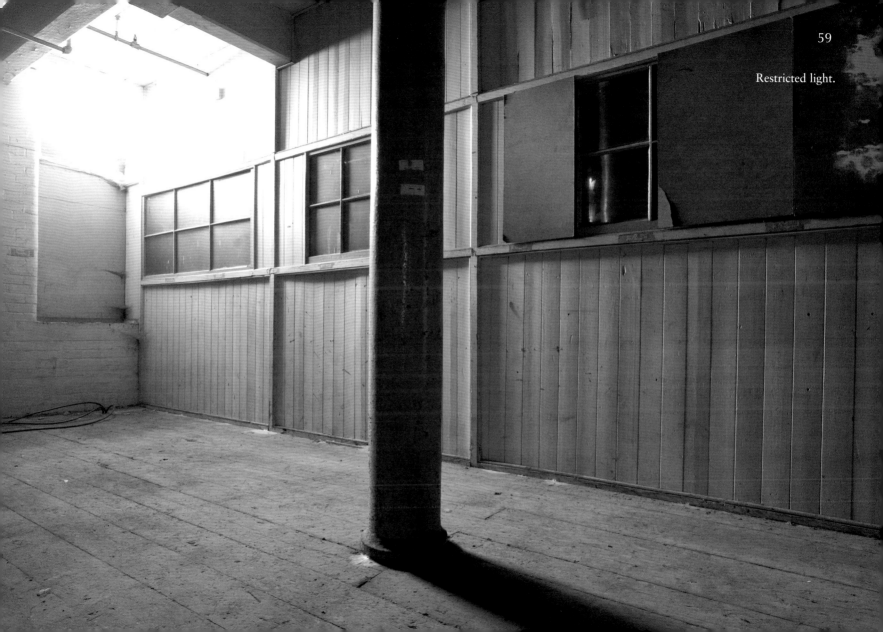

Restricted light.

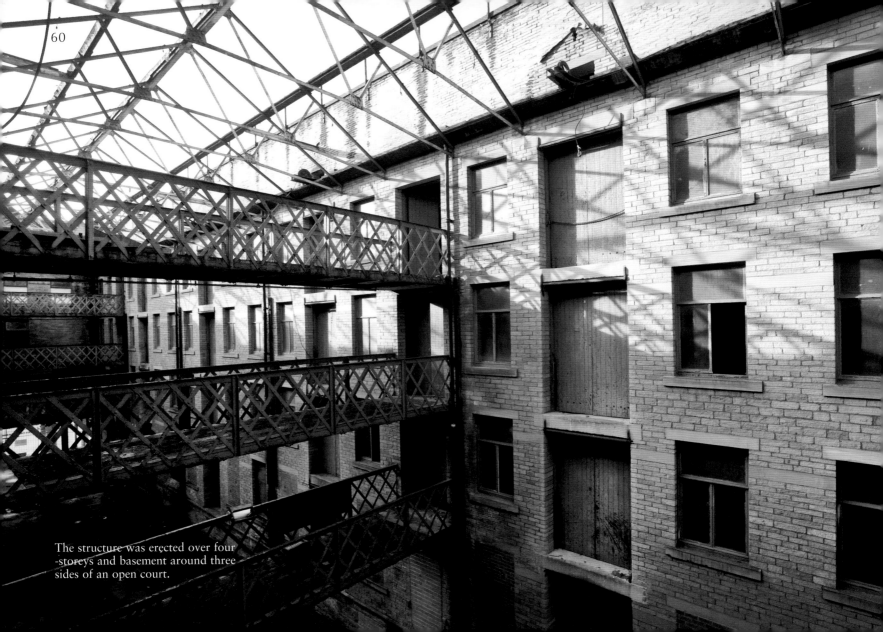

The structure was erected over four
-storeys and basement around three
sides of an open court.

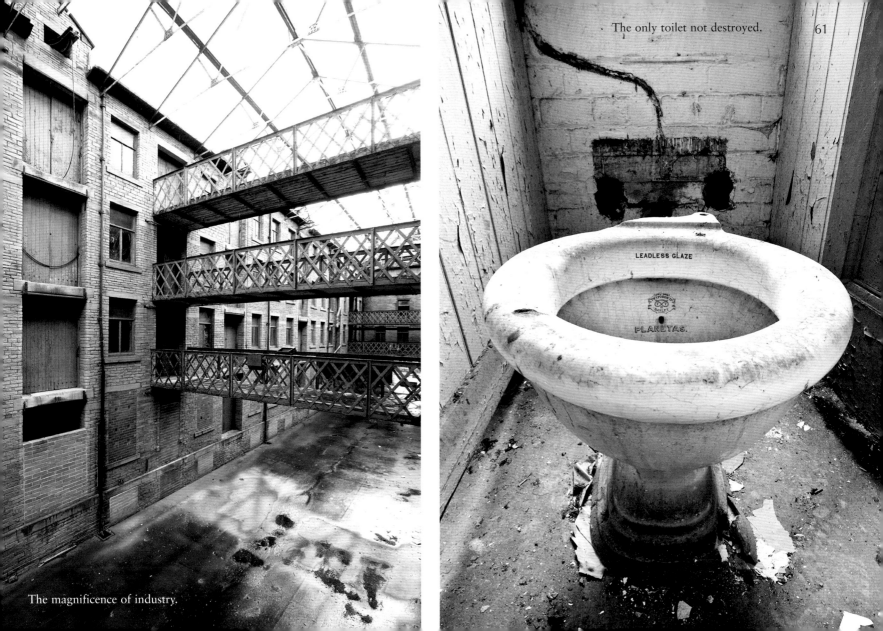

The magnificence of industry.

LEADLESS GLAZE

PLANETAS.

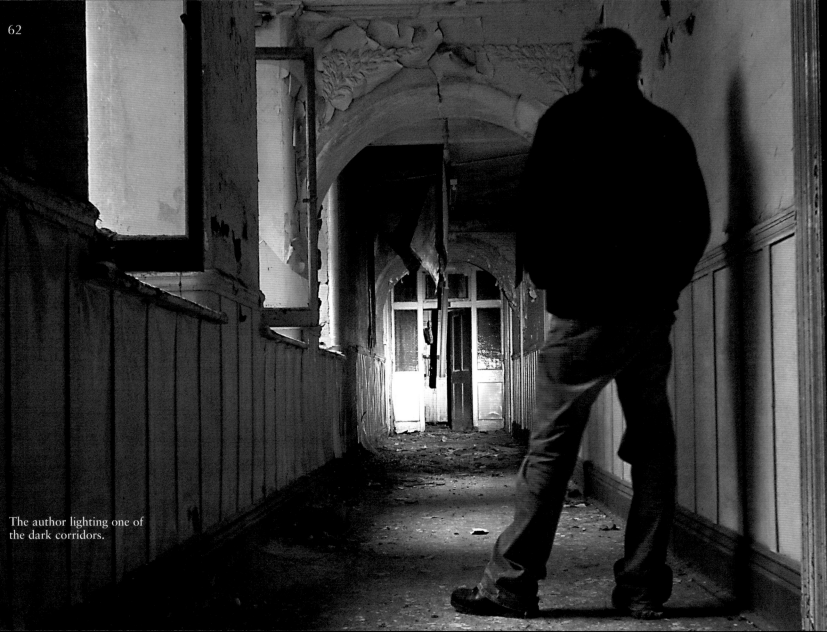

The author lighting one of
the dark corridors.

WAPPING SCHOOL

Wapping Road Board School was built in 1877 under Bradford's very own W. E. Forster's Education Act of 1870. The school's distinguished 123-year history saw it play a leading role in the development of state education. In the last year of the nineteenth century, it hit national and international headlines with the help of education campaigners Margaret and Rachel McMillan and their push to improve the lot of children in the state system. Their influence helped bring the country's first school swimming pool to Wapping Road School and nearby Green Lane School in 1899.

Bradford was a grim place for the poor in the nineteenth century, with extreme poverty commonplace. Children suffered in spite of the sacrifices made by their parents. Also at this time, children were brought up from the London workhouses to work in the mills. This is how the area of Wapping in Bradford originally got its name. Dirt and disease was an eternal problem. Right up to the early part of the last century some children were dressed for the winter in flannel, which was then sewn into place and not removed until the warm weather came. Parents thought that this was necessary because there was not enough food to keep a child warm otherwise. Hunger was the main problem and the effect of hunger on a child's education was a concern.

At Wapping Road School, in 1887, the headmaster, Mr W. H. Sykes, saw several children keel over and faint during morning assembly. He sent out for bread, jam and tea and paid for it from his own pocket, unwittingly serving the world's first free school meal.

Margaret and Rachel lived at No. 49 Hanover Square, off Manningham Lane towards the city centre end (1883–1902). A blue plaque marks the house and states, 'All children are mine'. Margaret McMillan was a champion of children.

A remarkable heritage that is in
serious danger of being lost forever.

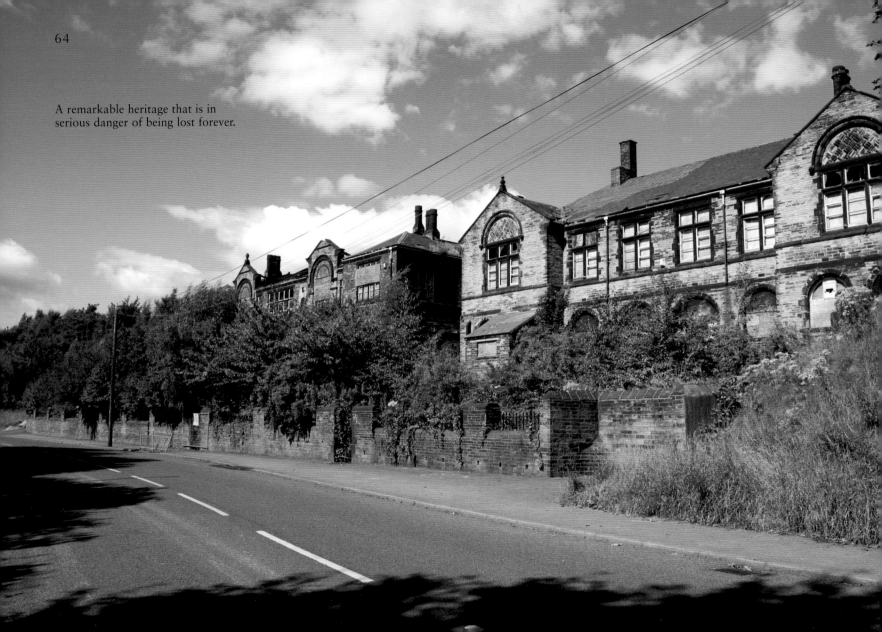

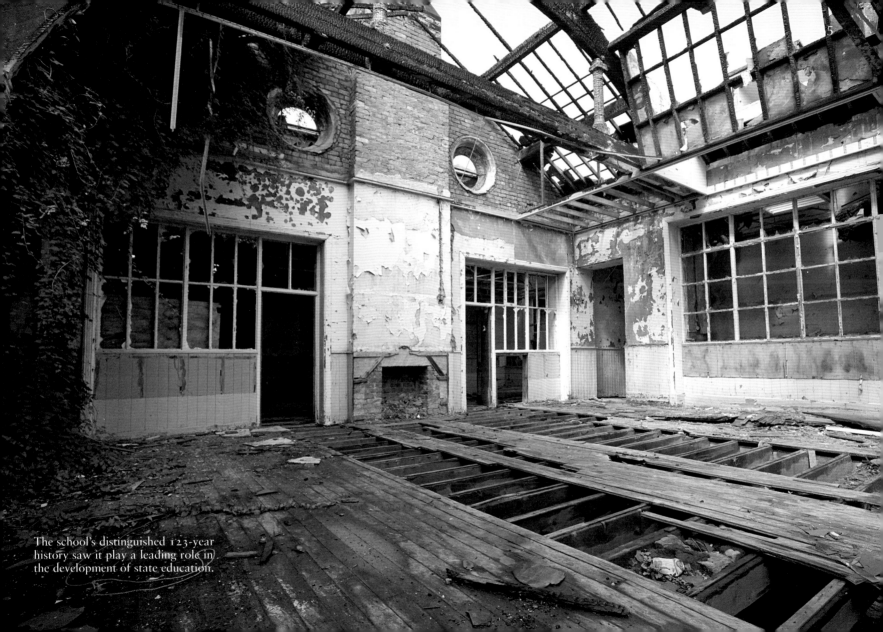

The school's distinguished 123-year history saw it play a leading role in the development of state education.

In June 2012, fire fighters were
once again called to the former First
School building in Wapping following
another attempt to destroy it.

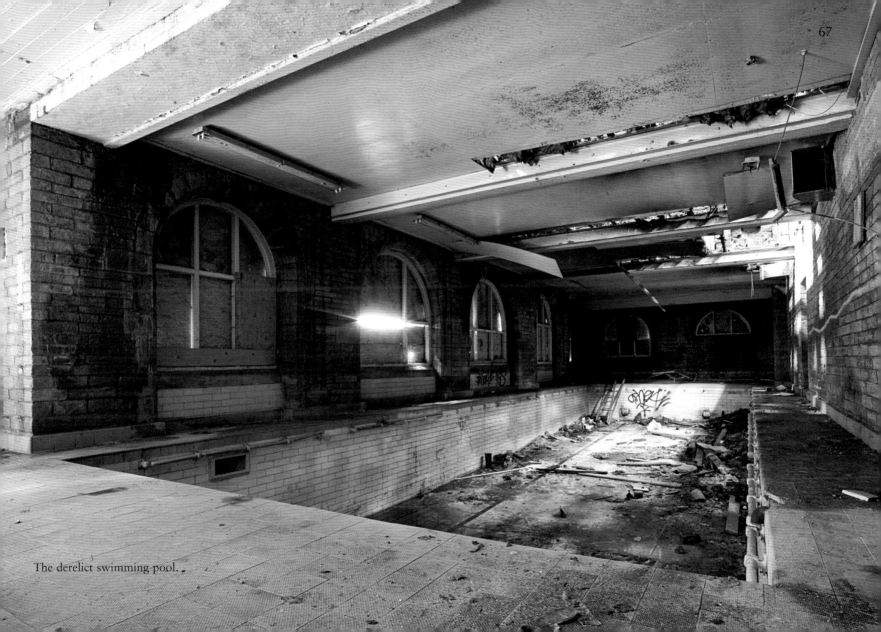

The derelict swimming pool.

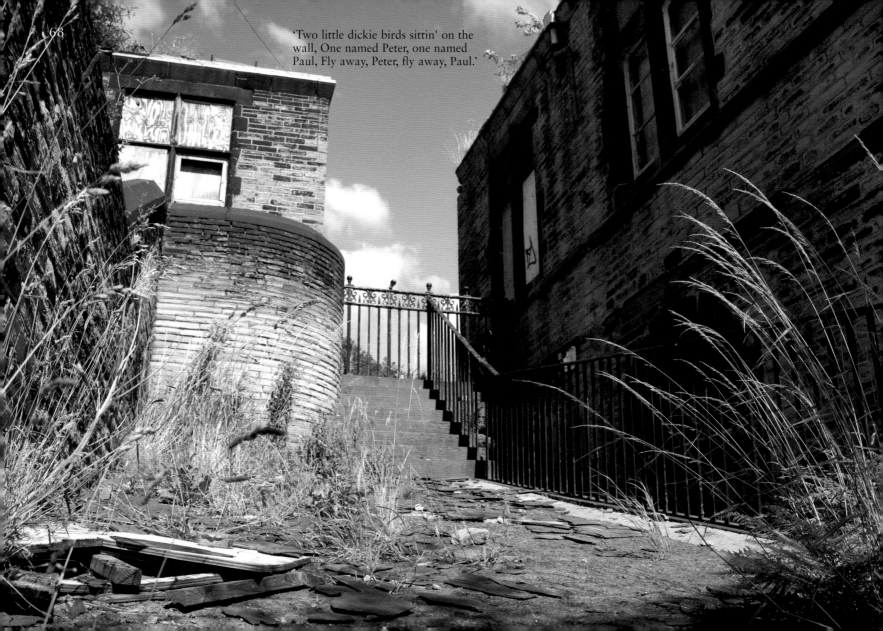

'Two little dickie birds sittin' on the wall, One named Peter, one named Paul, Fly away, Peter, fly away, Paul.'

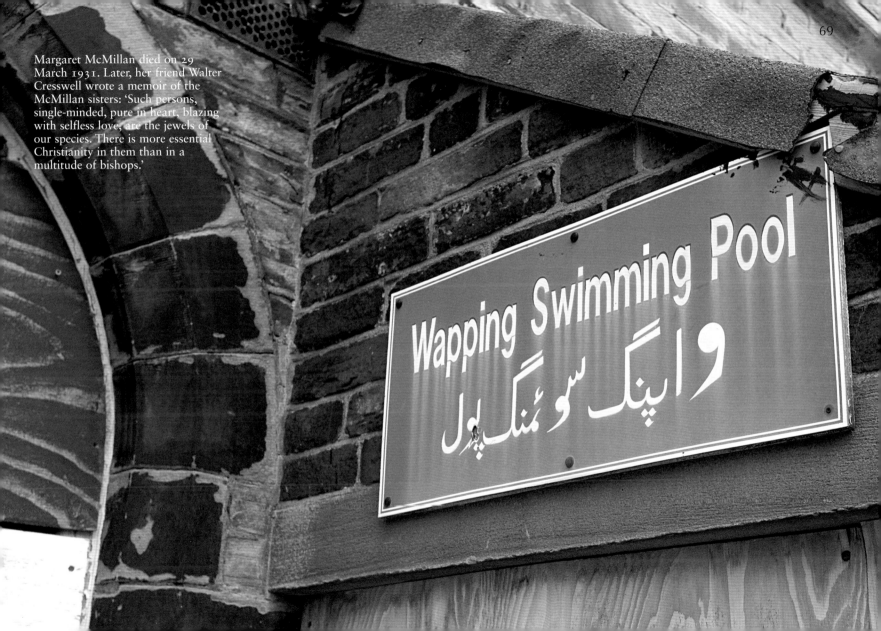

Margaret McMillan died on 29 March 1931. Later, her friend Walter Cresswell wrote a memoir of the McMillan sisters: 'Such persons, single-minded, pure in heart, blazing with selfless love, are the jewels of our species. There is more essential Christianity in them than in a multitude of bishops.'

Wapping Swimming Pool

واپنگ سوئمنگ پول

JOHN CRABTREE & SONS LTD

I can find very little information regarding this old mill located on the corner of Water Lane and Wigan Street. In the 1903 directory it lists the building as Davies, Edwards & Co., engineers Water Lane Works. Herman Spitz, a cloth weaver, is also identified as occupying a part of the site. Having located maps at Bradford Central Library, it would appear the development was built on the footprint of an old iron foundry. In later life John Crabtree & Sons made it their place of business. In more recent years it has been utilised as a garage and a chicken farm was located on the top floor. Evidence of John Crabtree and his work within the woollen industry are commonplace around the various floor levels. With regard to John Crabtree, the only worthy information found was in a roll call for the Bradford Pals in the Great War for the first 1,000 men to enlist in 1914. The list names one of the men as Lieutenant D. L. Crabtree, a son of the late John Crabtree, Bradford Wool Merchant. This may not be our John Crabtree but possibly his father, as sons were often called in their father's name.

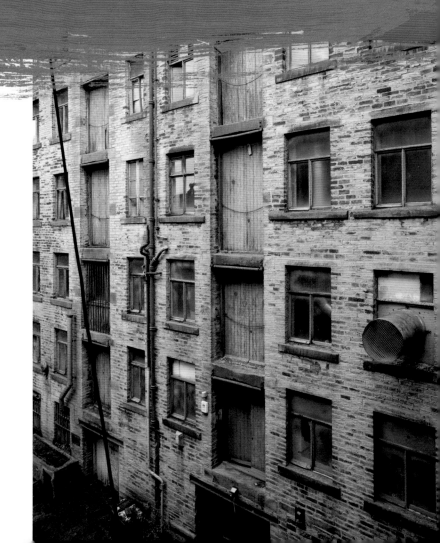

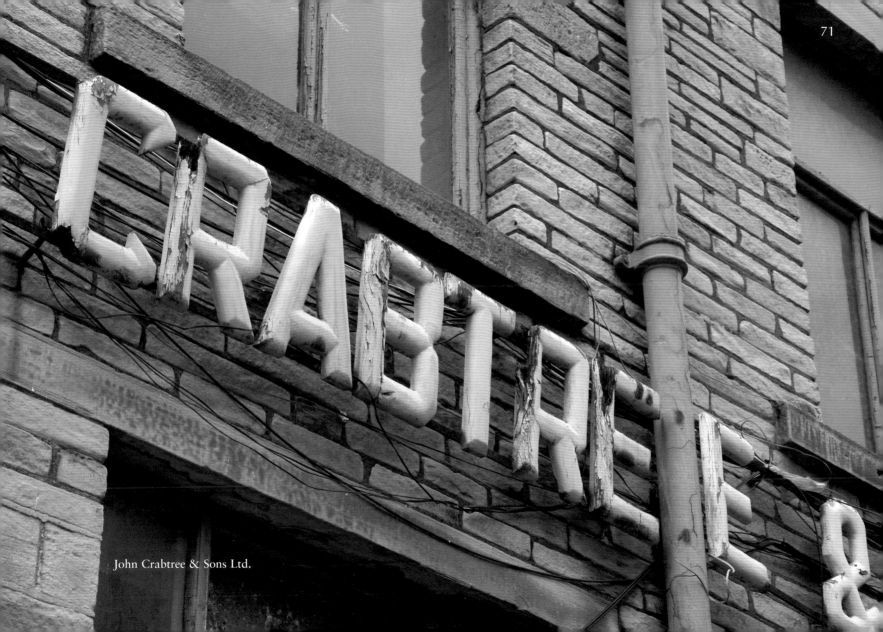

John Crabtree & Sons Ltd.

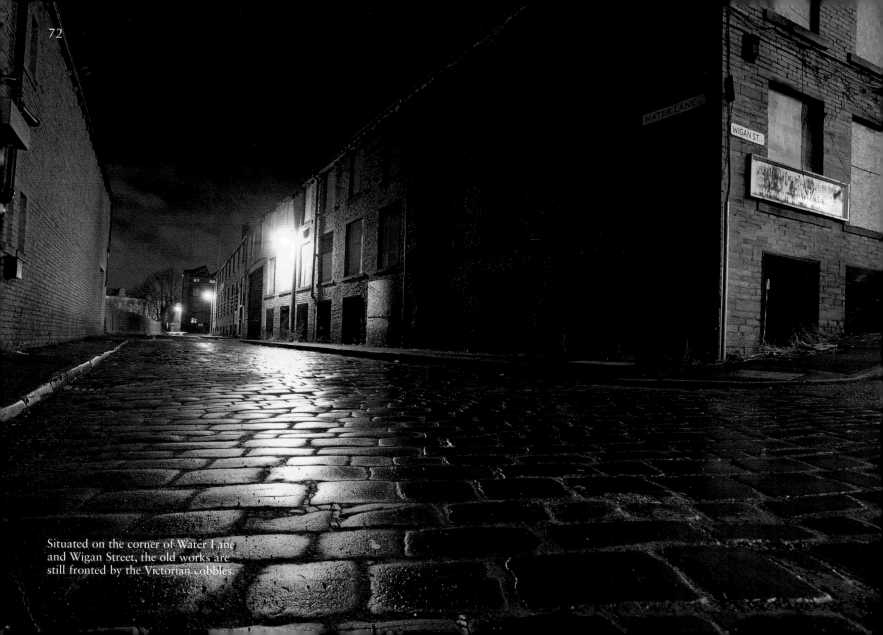

Situated on the corner of Water Lane
and Wigan Street, the old works are
still fronted by the Victorian cobbles.

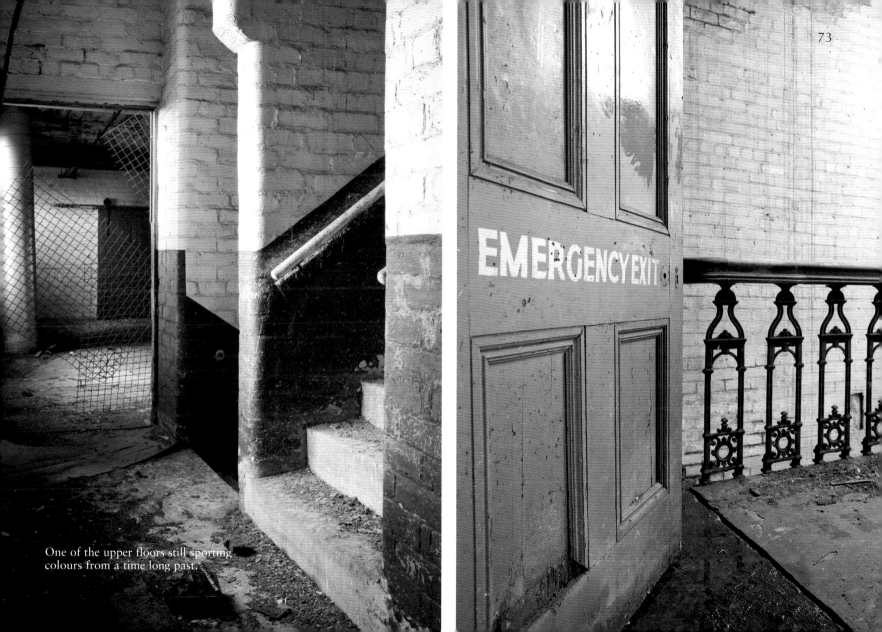

One of the upper floors still sporting colours from a time long past.

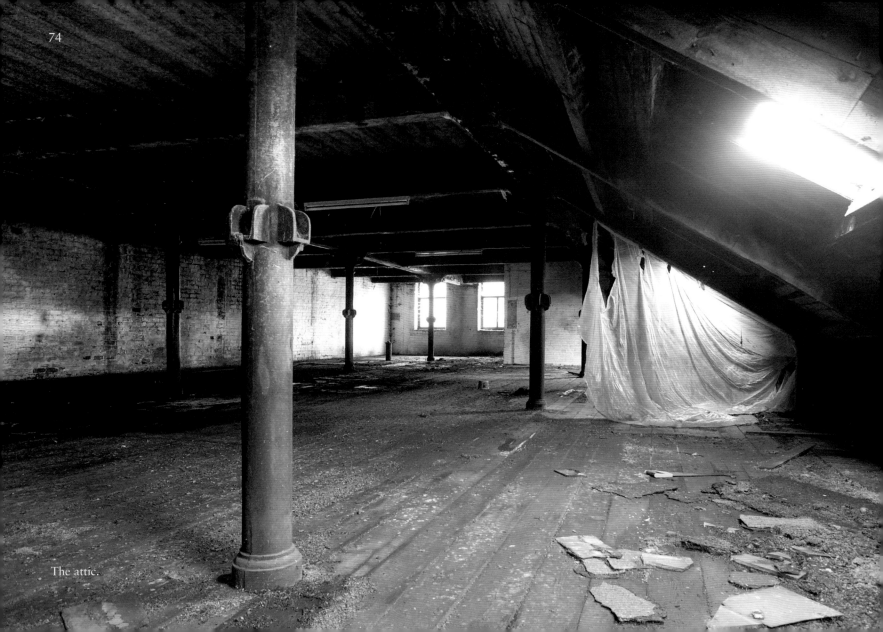

The attic.

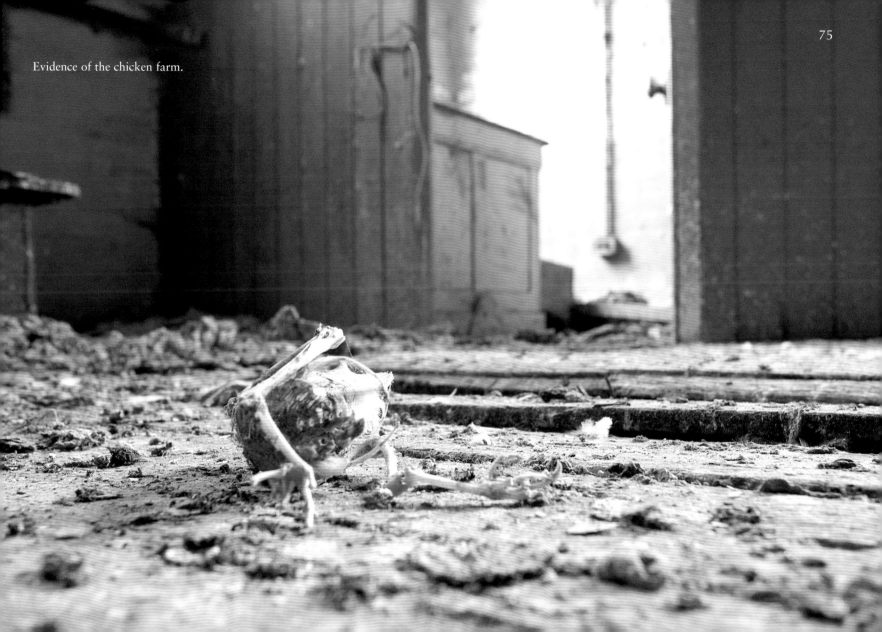

Evidence of the chicken farm.

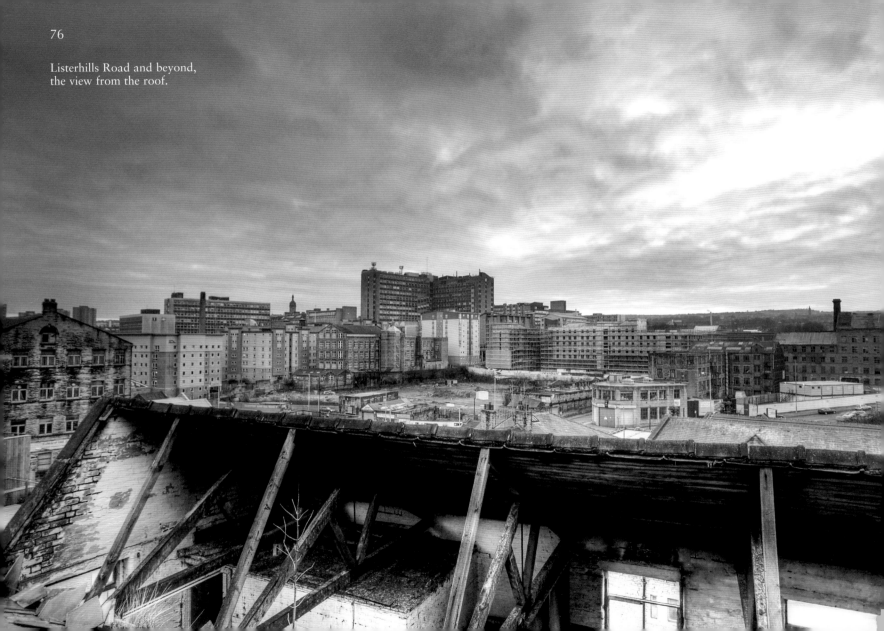

Listerhills Road and beyond,
the view from the roof.

MIDLAND MILLS

Designed by Williams Andrews and Joseph Pepper in 1871, Midland Mills on Cape Street was the first mill the partnership were commissioned to draw up the plans for. Later, the duo would also design Manningham Mills, Bradford Fever Hospital and the Grammar School on Manor Row to name a few. Until 2001 the mill was occupied by British Mohair Spinners, which is represented by the goat-topped weather vane on one of the towers. The vast complex has in recent years been partly demolished and stripped internally ready for a £35 million redevelopment . In 2010 Councillors gave a conditional green light to the scheme, which had stalled during the recession. Members of the authority's Regulatory & Appeals Committee unanimously approved an application to convert three Grade II listed buildings at Midland Mills, Valley Road, into apartments and build two residential buildings and parking spaces. Tony Lupton, managing director of Beckwith Design Associates Ltd, which was also behind the development, said he hoped the scheme would be completed within three years. Despite the 2010 agreement, in 2014 the mill remains in a derelict state as depicted in these images.

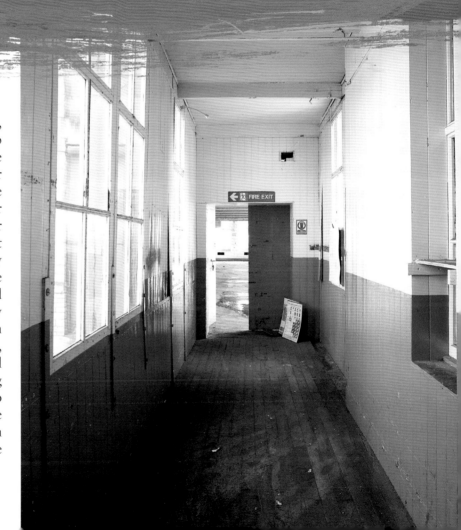

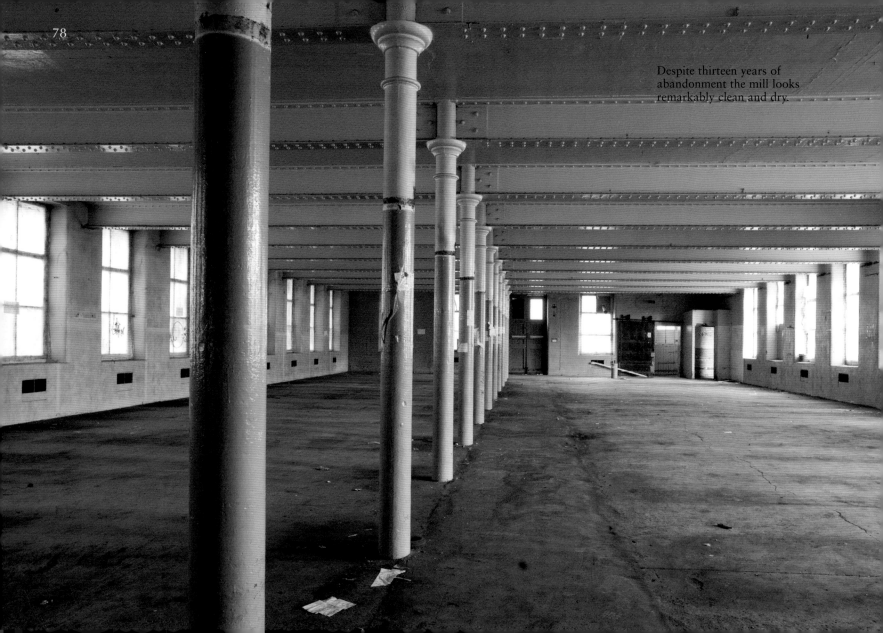

Despite thirteen years of
abandonment the mill looks
remarkably clean and dry.

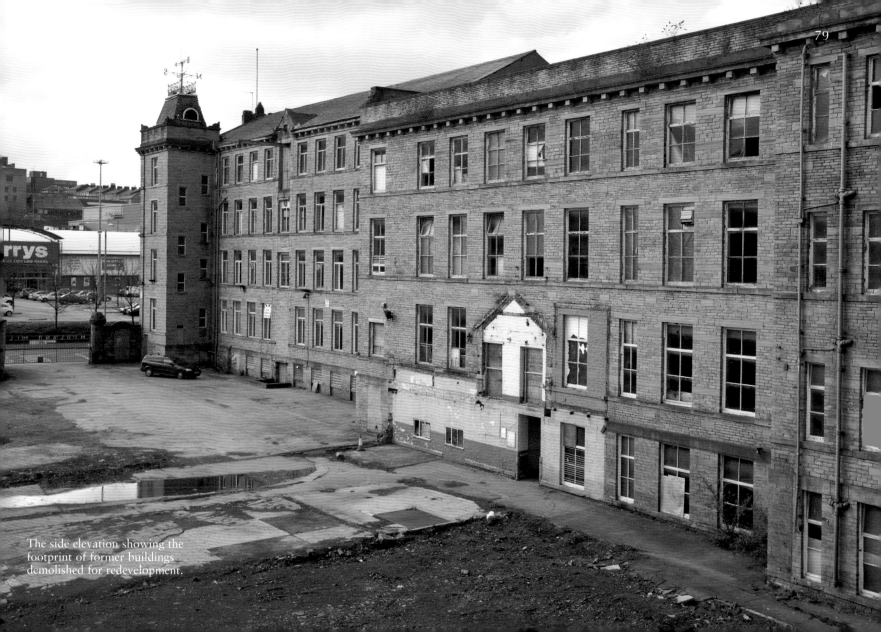

The side elevation showing the footprint of former buildings demolished for redevelopment.

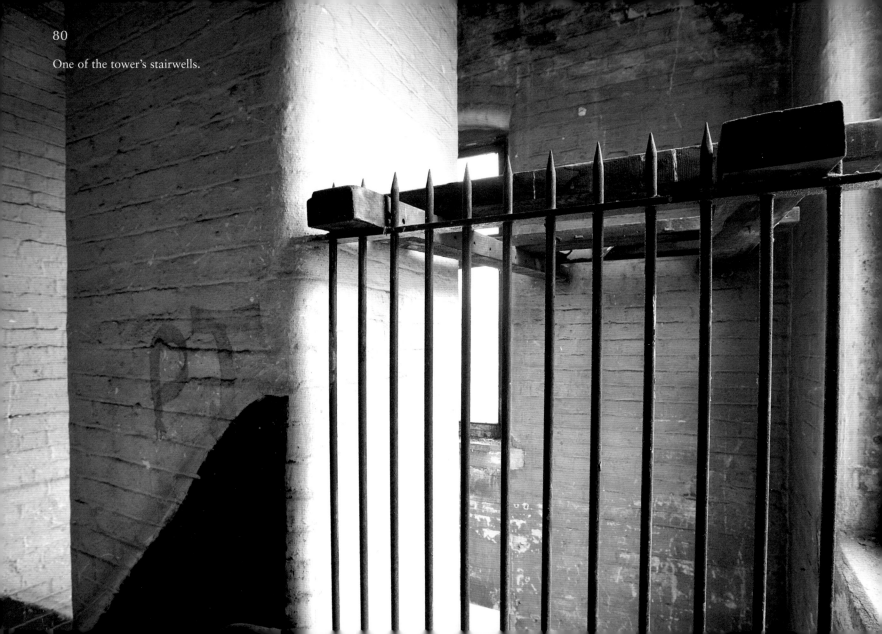

One of the tower's stairwells.

ST MARY'S CATHOLIC CHURCH

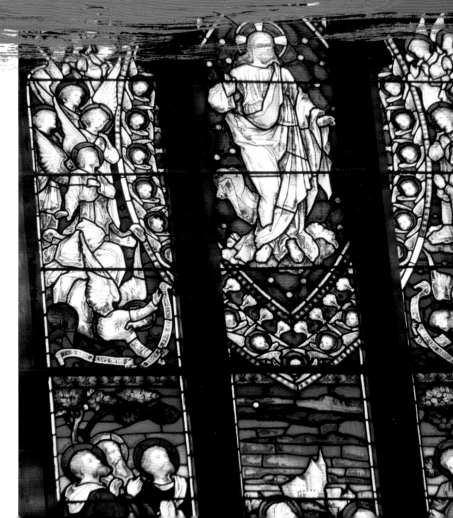

Built to the designs of Edward Simpson (1844–1937) in 1872, St Mary's did not open her doors to the congregation till 1876. Simpson was renowned for almost exclusively designing Roman Catholic churches which were often bizarre or grotesque but always felt to be his individual interpretations of the Gothic style. In 1976, upon the centenary of the opening, it was reported that around 1,100 people took Mass every Sunday. By 2006 proposals for closing half the district's Catholic churches were revealed exclusively to the Bradford *Telegraph & Argus* by Bishop Roche, when he said the closure plans were due to the natural decline in the number of priests and a drop in the number of churchgoers as well as crumbling buildings. Monsignor Michael McQuinn, the Vicar General for the diocese, said, 'These are pastoral decisions and are made for church reasons. We want to maintain our city centre presence but no longer feel that we have the resources to keep St Mary's open.' Today, in 2014, the church with all its fittings is closed to the public but is usefully employed in the storage of food for the city's homeless.

The front elevation showing the Priest
accommodation to the right.

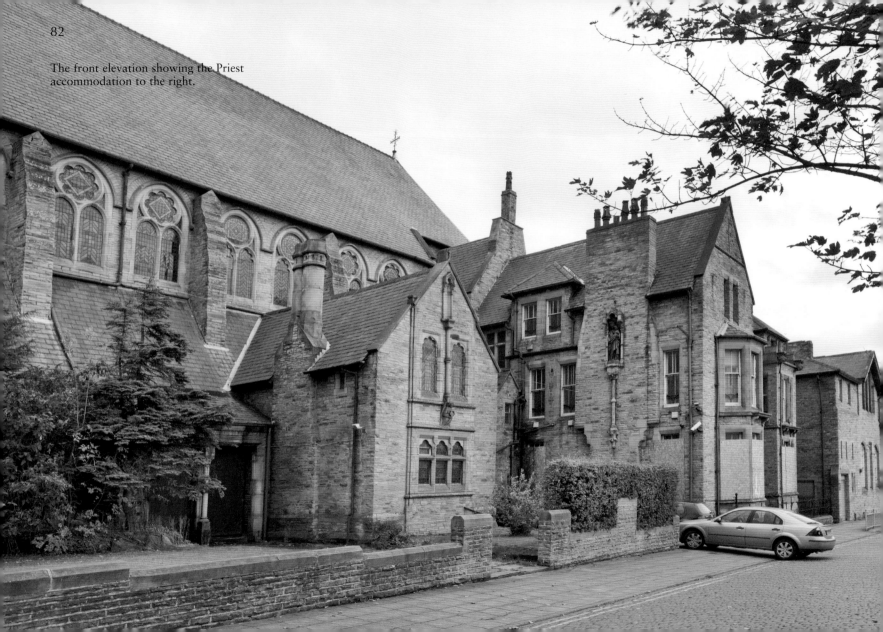

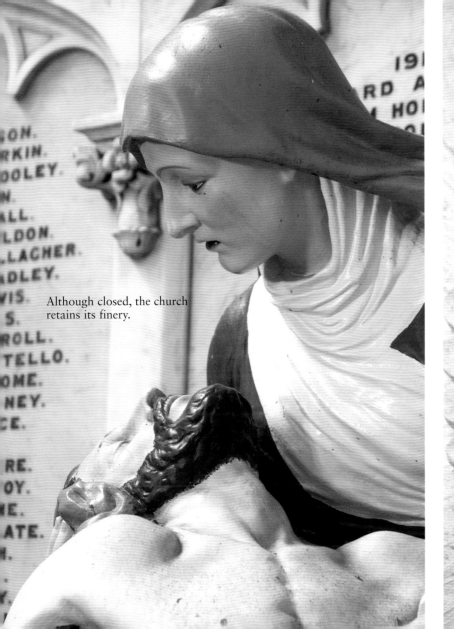

Although closed, the church retains its finery.

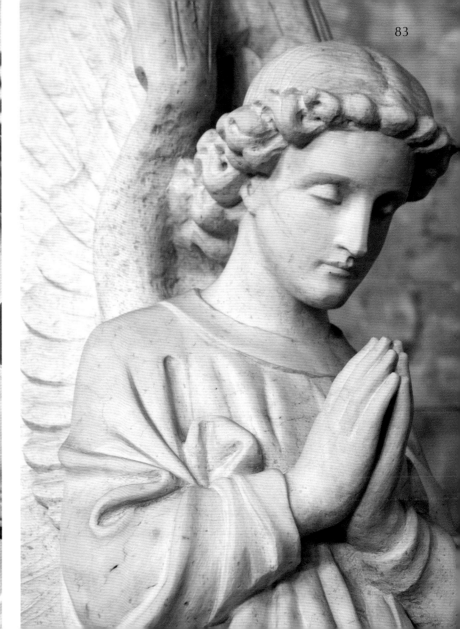

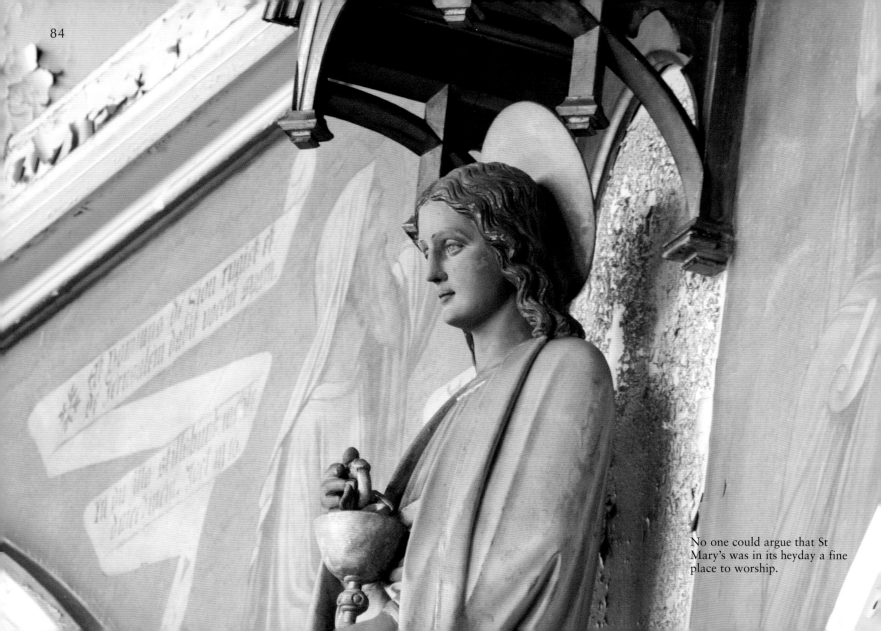

No one could argue that St Mary's was in its heyday a fine place to worship.

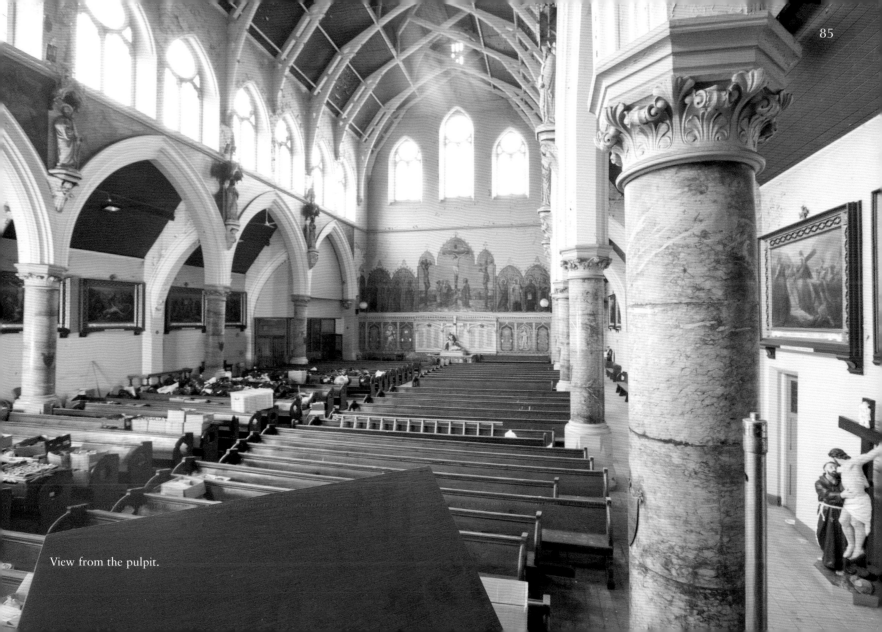

View from the pulpit.

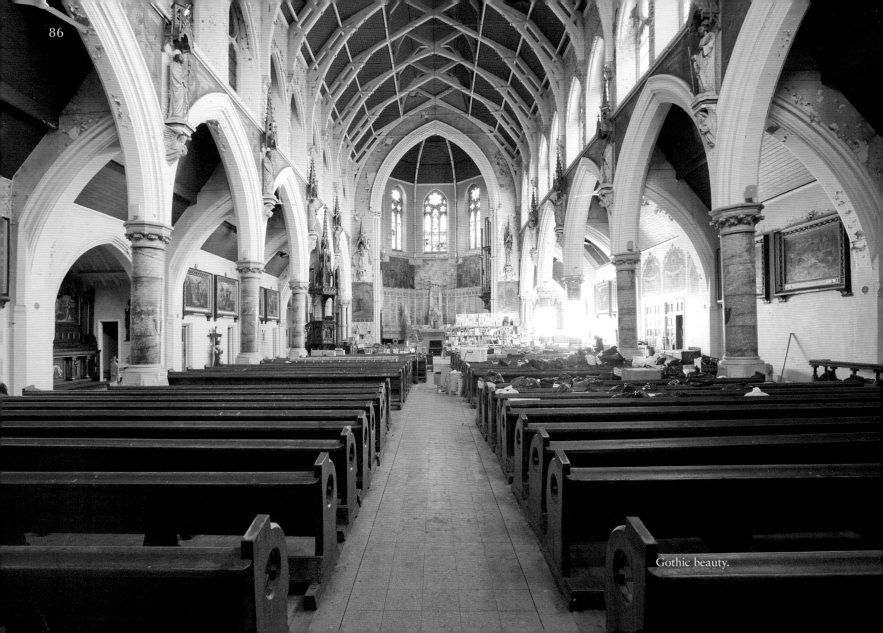

Gothic beauty.

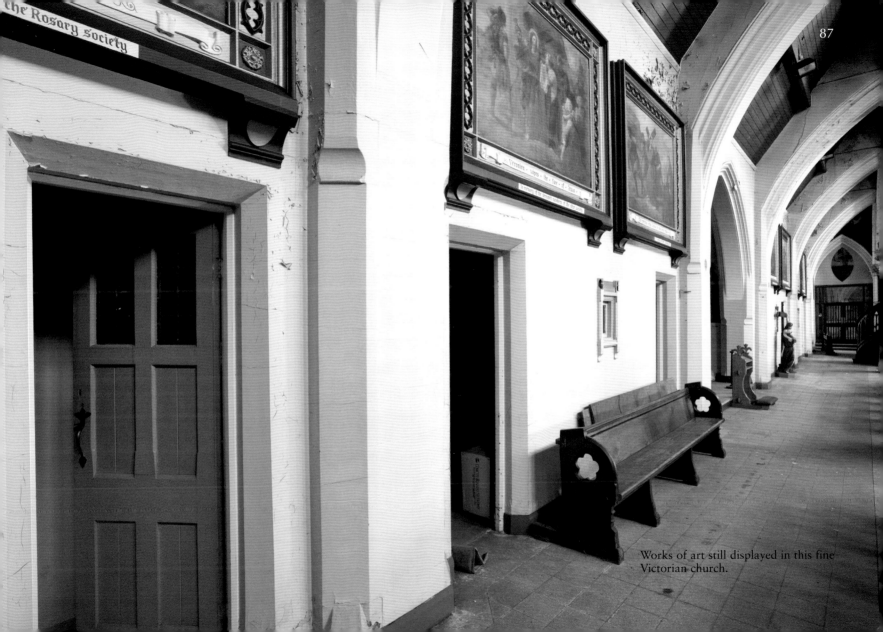

Works of art still displayed in this fine Victorian church.

THOMPSONS MILL

Prior to the fire that ripped through this wonderful old mill it was thought to be the second oldest mill surviving in Bradford. Built in the very early part of the nineteenth century by a Mr Piele, it was later, in the 1830s, owned by Matthew and Benjamin Thompson. Matthew Thompson, who would become Sir Matthew Thompson, was the father of Alderman Matthew William Thompson (1820–91), the mayor of Bradford 1861/62 and 1871–73. It was during the latter term that he opened the town hall, designed by architects Lockwood & Mawson, on 9 September 1873, with a large bell named in his honour. Over the years, the mill, which was located by the new Provident building at Goitside, has been known by many names, including Bradfax and more recently Molletts catering.

From the *Telegraph & Argus* 10 October 2011:

'A blaze which destroyed one of Bradford's oldest mills was started deliberately, fire chiefs confirmed today. The fire ripped through the five storeys of Thompson Mill in Tetley Street, off Thornton Road, last week, leaving it so badly damaged that it had to be demolished. Traffic was brought to a standstill as firefighters fought the blaze last Tuesday night. Crews were able to prevent it spreading to nearby properties but could not save the mill. Fire investigation officer, Station Manager Richard Hagger, confirmed the fire had been started deliberately. He said the fire was believed to have been started in rubbish and other materials on the first floor. Mr Hagger said it was most likely that a match or lighter was used.

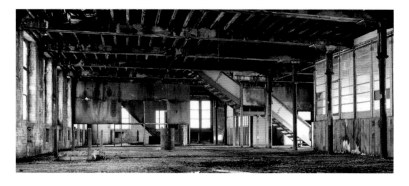

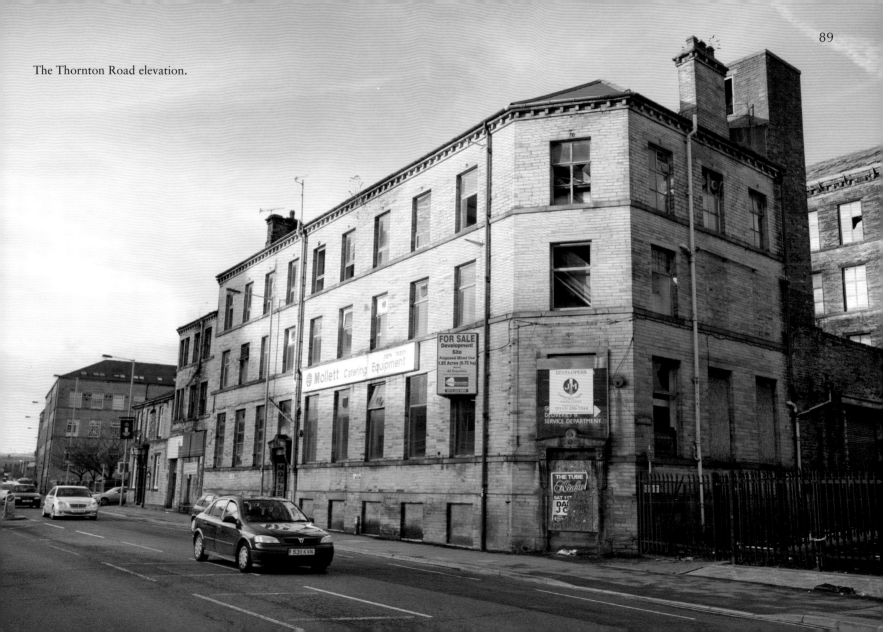

The Thornton Road elevation.

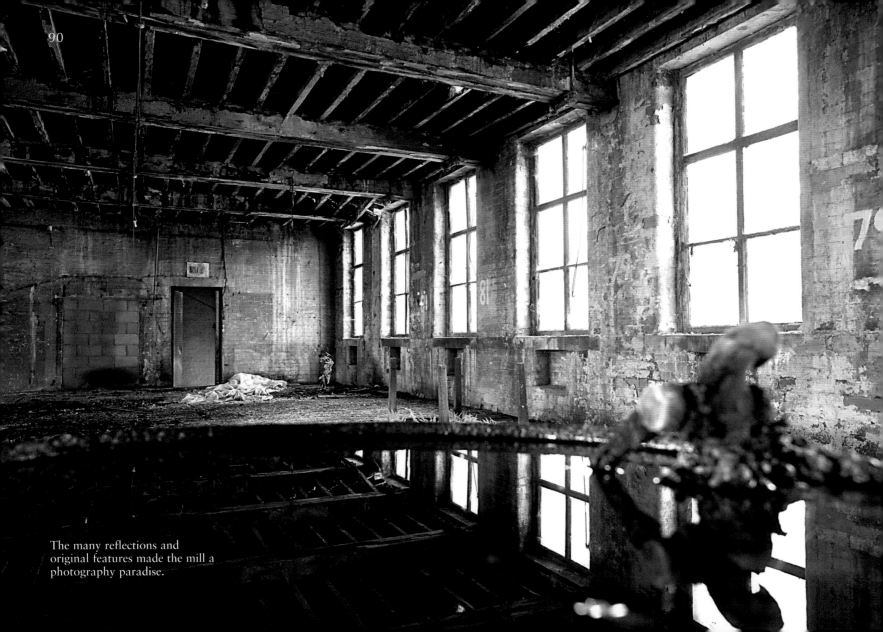

The many reflections and
original features made the mill a
photography paradise.

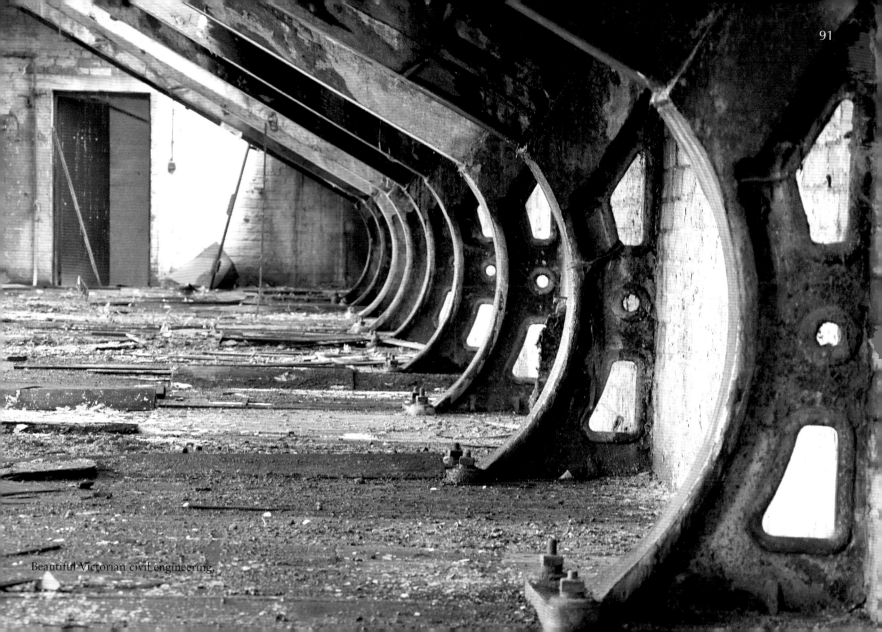

Beautiful Victorian civil engineering.

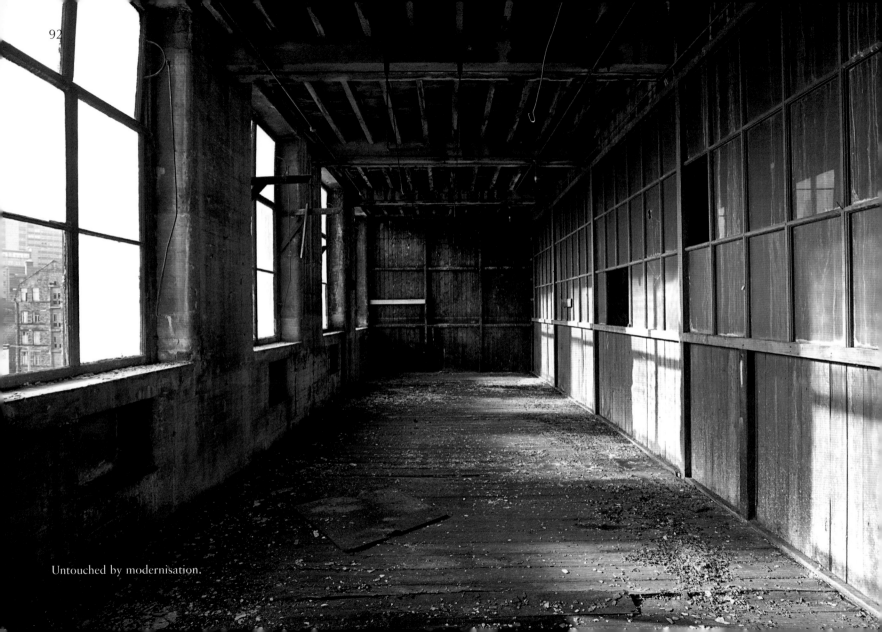

Untouched by modernisation.

principal entrance or entrances
h parts as an inspector may direct.

FACTORIES ACT 1961

RMISSIBLE HOURS OF

(APART FROM "OVERTIME")
STATUTORY INTERVALS AND HOLIDAYS FOR WOMEN AND YOUNG

Form of Notice prescribed in pursuance of sections 88, 115 and 138, Factories Act 1961

notice that the periods of employment and statutory intervals for meals and rest will be as shown in the Table belo
from the 1st June, 1964.

, to avail myself of the Special Exception(s) in the following section

*Delete where not required.

Name of Occupier   BRADFAX LIMITED.

Signature of
Occupier or Agent

Address of Factory   FULTON STREET,

OFF THORNTON ROAD, BRADFORD..

Date

Remnants of an
industrial life.

Monday	Tuesday	Wednesday	Thursday	Friday	Saturday	In E
From a.m.	To	From	To	From	To	given

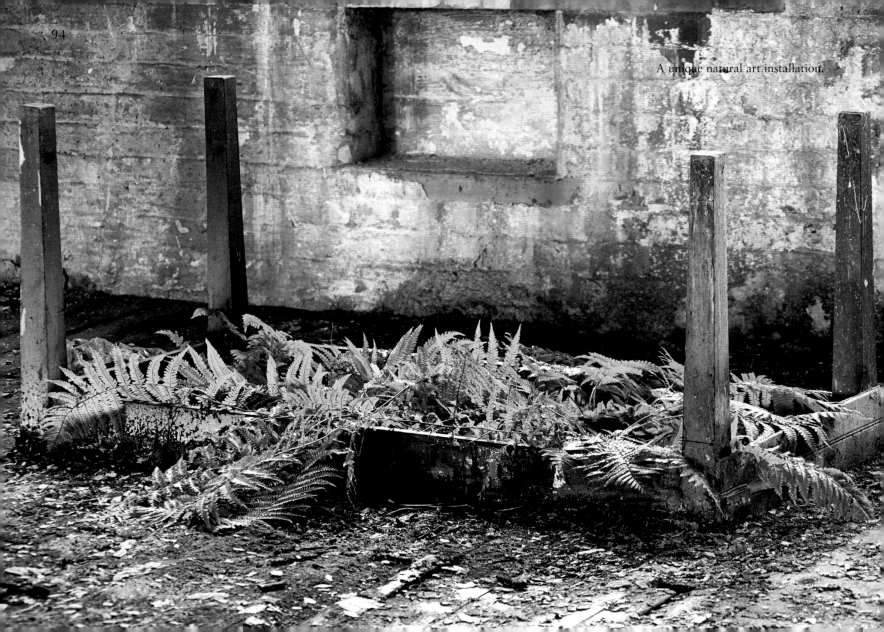

A unique natural art installation.

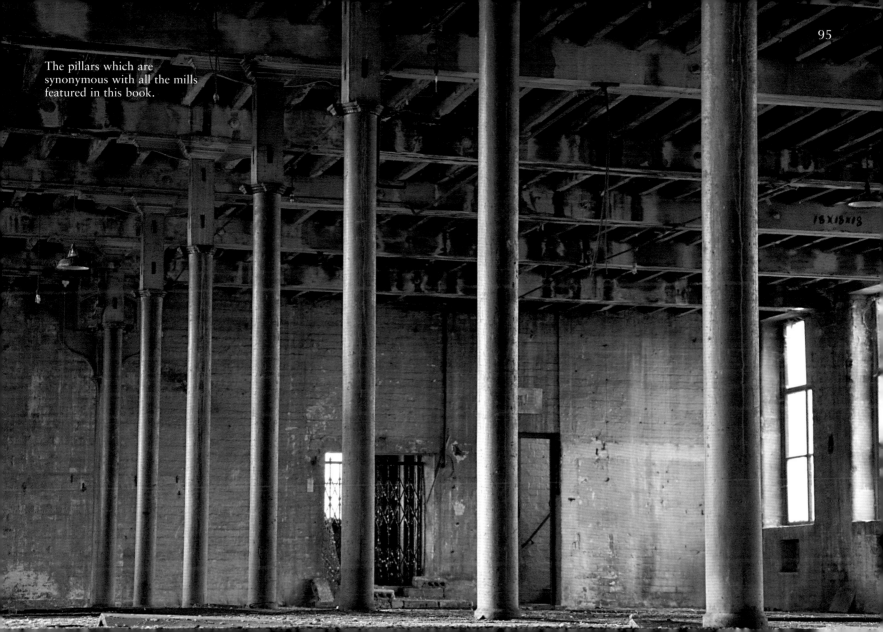

The pillars which are synonymous with all the mills featured in this book.

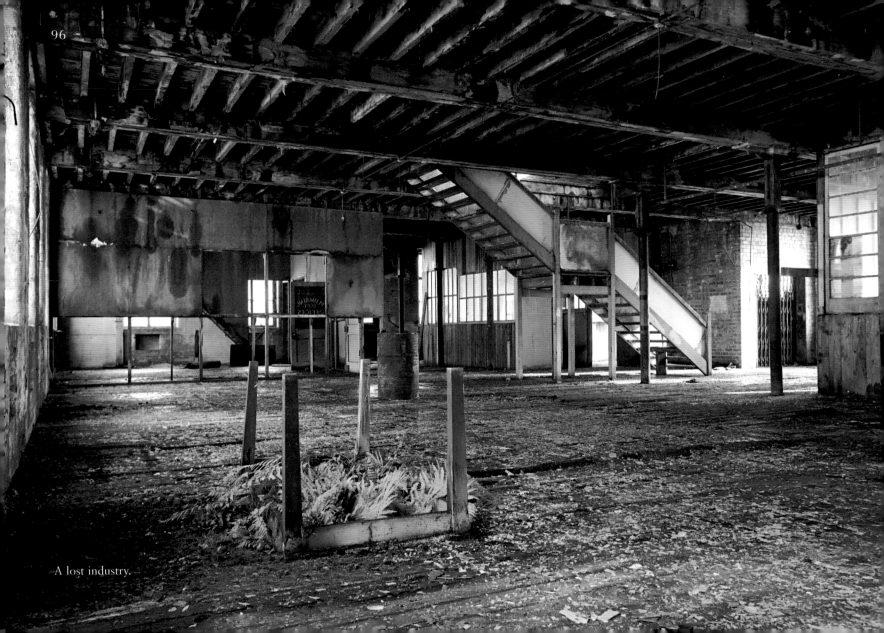

A lost industry.

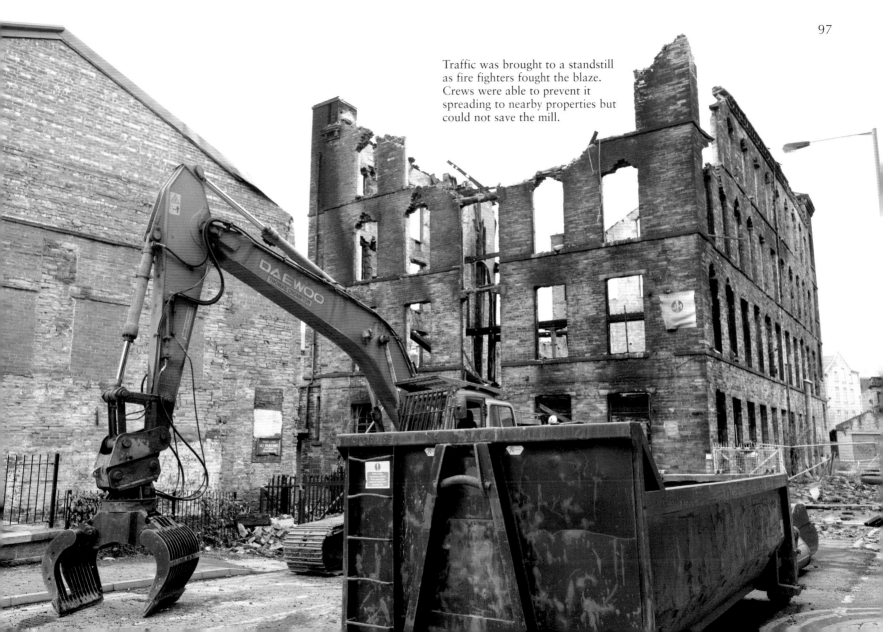

Traffic was brought to a standstill as fire fighters fought the blaze. Crews were able to prevent it spreading to nearby properties but could not save the mill.

FAIRMOUNT PARK NURSING HOME

The Victorian semi-detached villas pictured here were, in Bradford's heyday, the comfortable homes of the more affluent of the city's residents. For example, in 1903, the house to the left was owned by J. W. Smith, who ran a spinning mill, while No. 15 next door was the residence of Lady Hannah Cass. Around this time, the Manningham district was the exclusive place to live in Bradford, with St Paul's Road being the very best postal address. At some point the two houses were converted into one residence, possibly to facilitate the formation of Fairmount Park Residential Home. What is interesting about this former nursing home is that, in many ways, it appears that staff and residents quite literally just left one day, leaving furniture and personal possessions behind much like the Mary Celeste. Clearly empty for some years, damp and neglect have taken their toll, with some of the ceilings collapsing in the bedrooms and communal areas. If ever there was a building that felt like a real haunted house then it is this one.

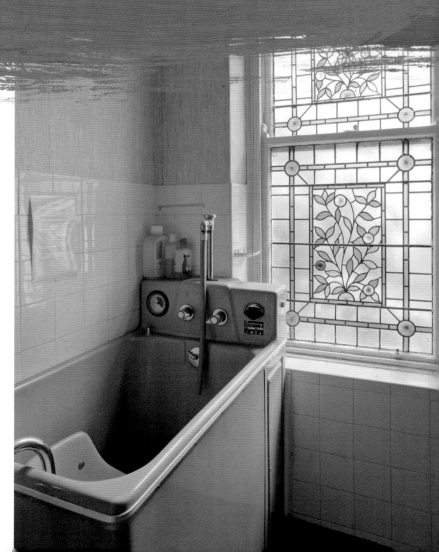

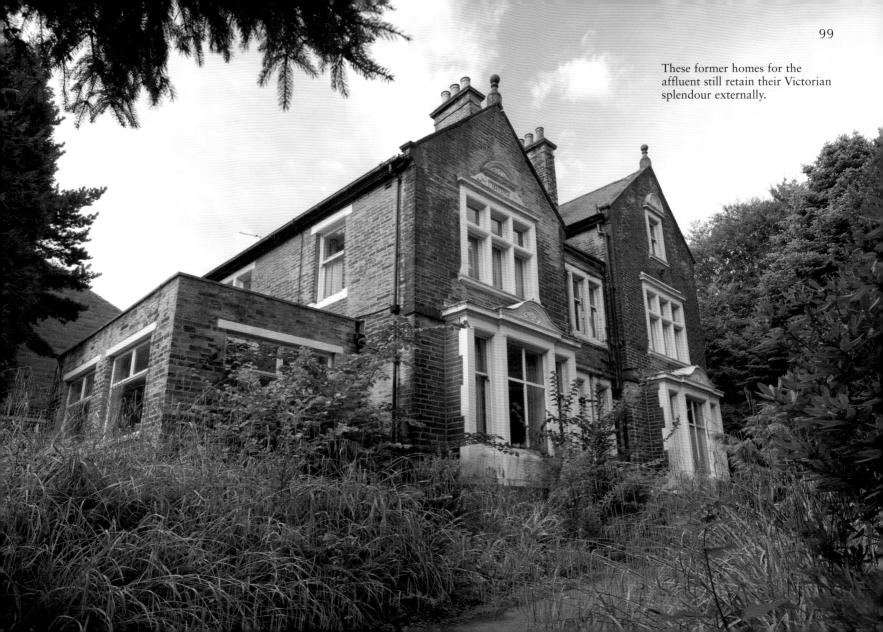

These former homes for the affluent still retain their Victorian splendour externally.

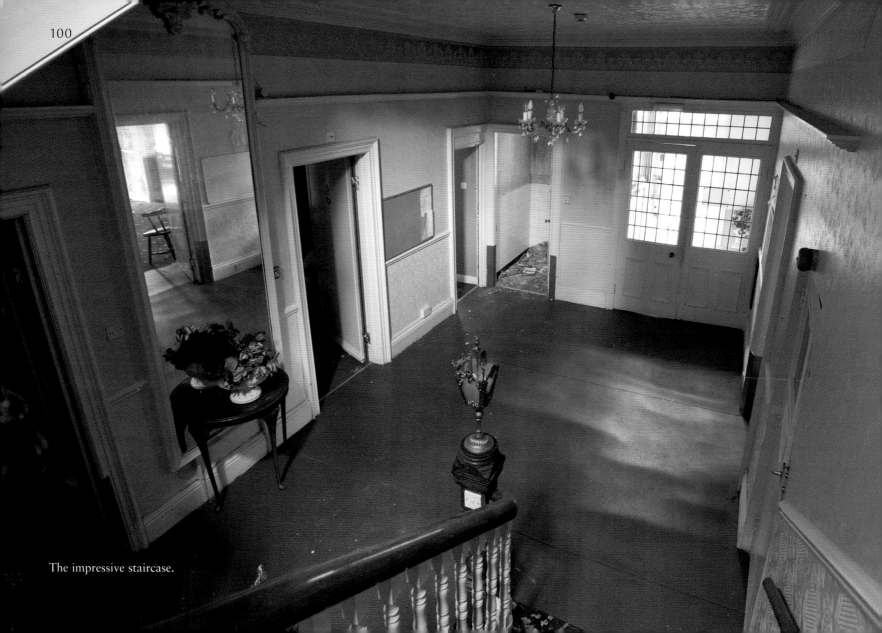

The impressive staircase.

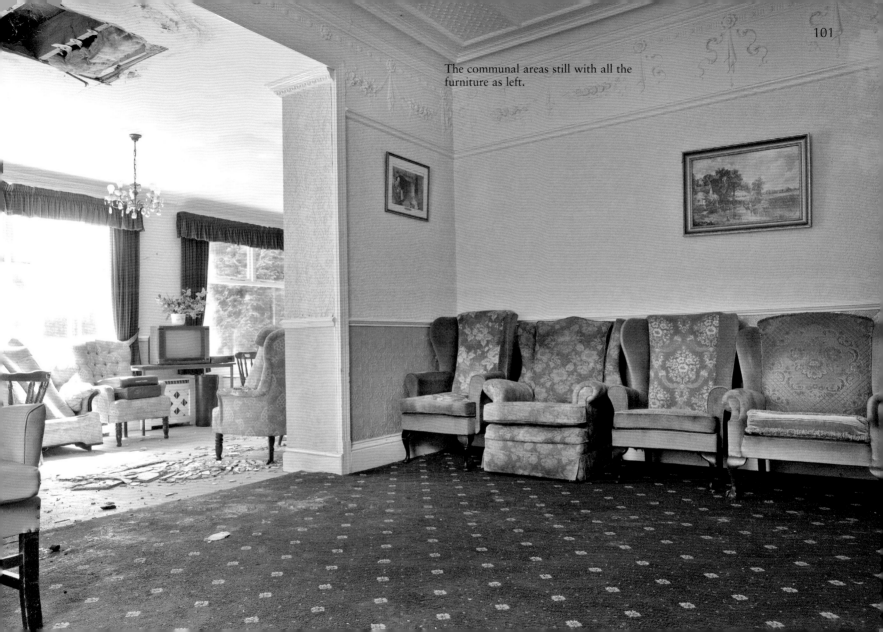

The communal areas still with all the furniture as left.

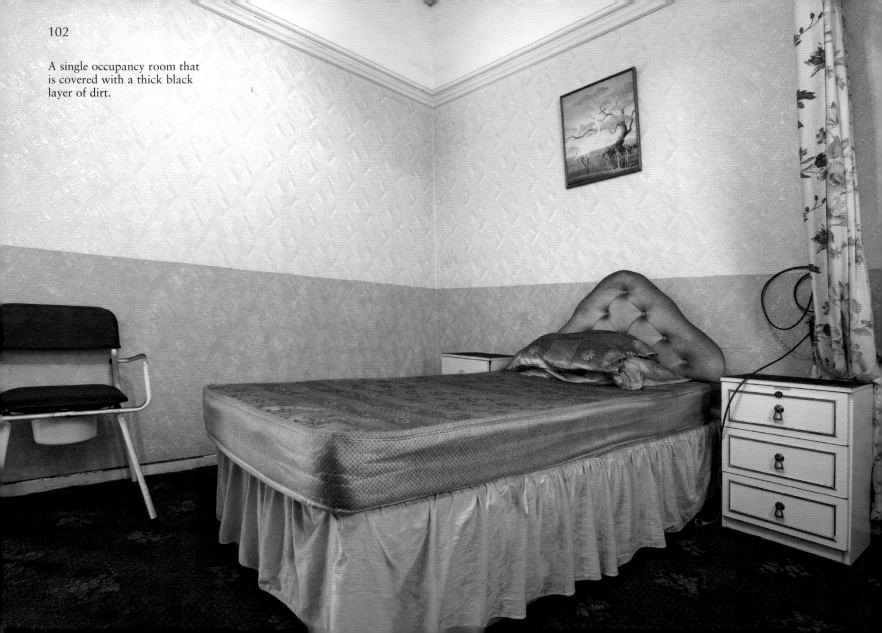

A single occupancy room that is covered with a thick black layer of dirt.

WEST BOWLING MORTUARY CHAPEL

This little Victorian chapel would have been used just prior to the burial service. At one point there would have been two chapels just as at Undercliffe Cemetery servicing both the Anglican and non-conformist burials. The chapel is quite literally falling down; however, it does retain some nice features, including the tiles, carved stonework and the original pews, although they are in short supply and rotting away. Like many of buildings featured in this book, there have been attempts to burn it down. Given its current state it is unlikely to be restored in the future.

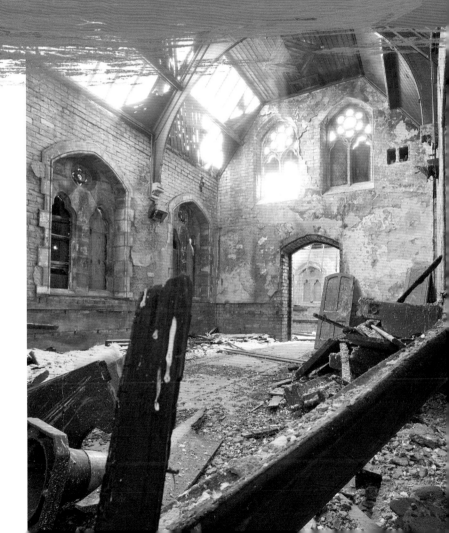

Right: The interior of the chapel.

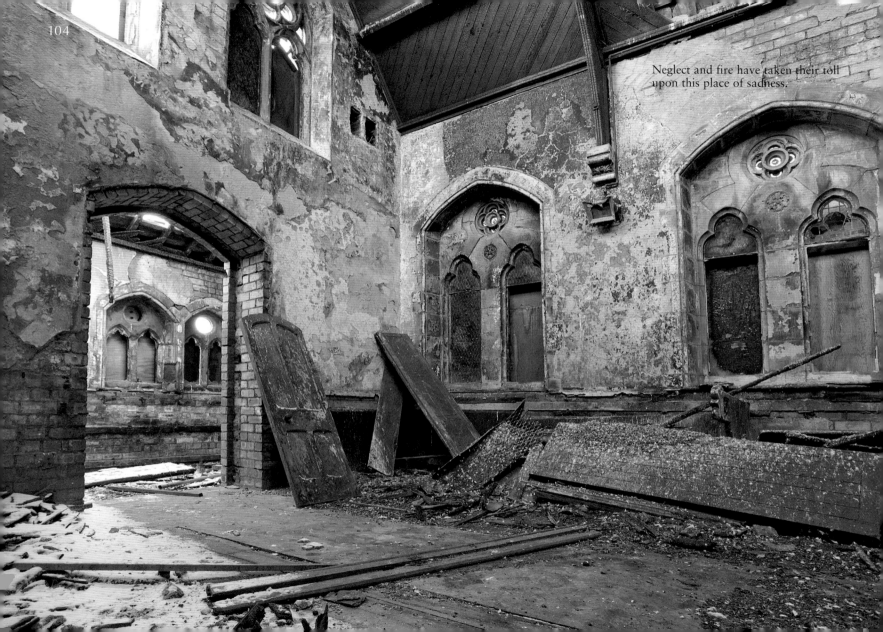

Neglect and fire have taken their toll upon this place of sadness.

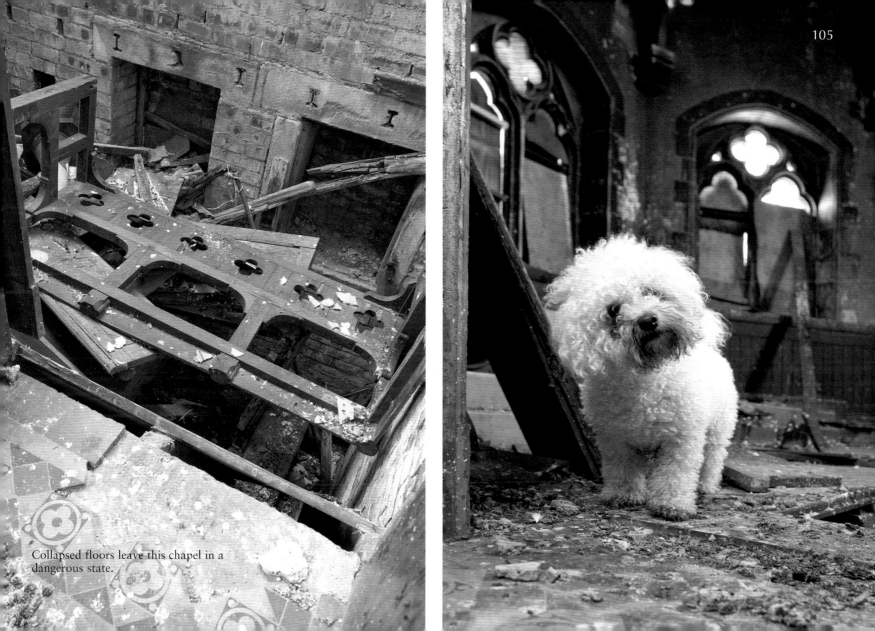

Collapsed floors leave this chapel in a dangerous state.

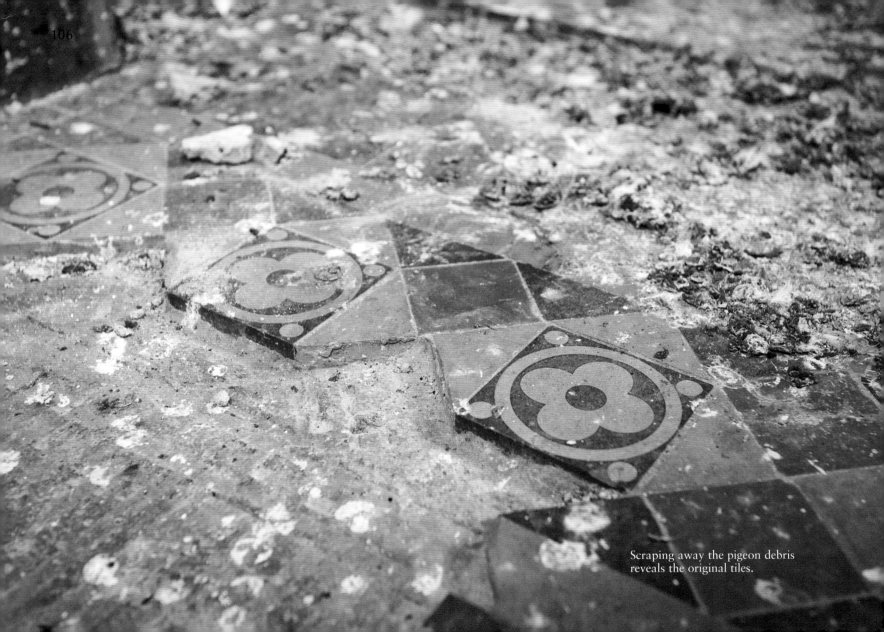

Scraping away the pigeon debris
reveals the original tiles.

LISTERS MILL

If there is one iconic mill in Bradford that truly dominates the skyline, then it is Manningham Mills, also known as Listers Mill. It was said at the time of building the 255-foot-high chimney that a man could drive a horse and cart around the top it was that wide. Much like in death, where the great industrialists competed for the best position on the promenade and most magnificent memorial stone at Undercliffe Cemetery, in life they competed with mills and especially the size of the chimneys.

The mill, which was completed in 1873 for Samuel Cunliffe Lister, was the largest silk factory in the world. Designed by architects William Andrews and Joseph Pepper in an Italianate style, the structure at its height employed some 11,000 men, women, and children. During the Second World War, Listers produced 1,330 miles of real parachute silk, 284 miles of flame-proof wool, 50 miles of khaki battledress and 4,430 miles of parachute cord for the war effort. A changing international economy saw the decline of the mill, and its eventual closure in 1992. The empty building then rapidly fell into decay and dereliction. In 2001, some nine years later, the site was purchased by property developers Urban Splash 2001, who, with assistance from Yorkshire Forward & Bradford Council, started converting the Silk Mill into apartments. Although much has already been converted there is still a large area left awaiting regeneration.

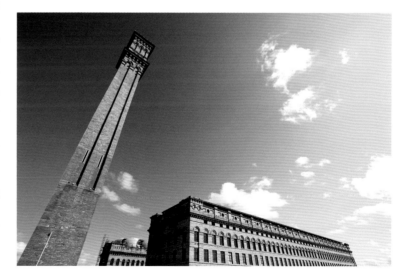

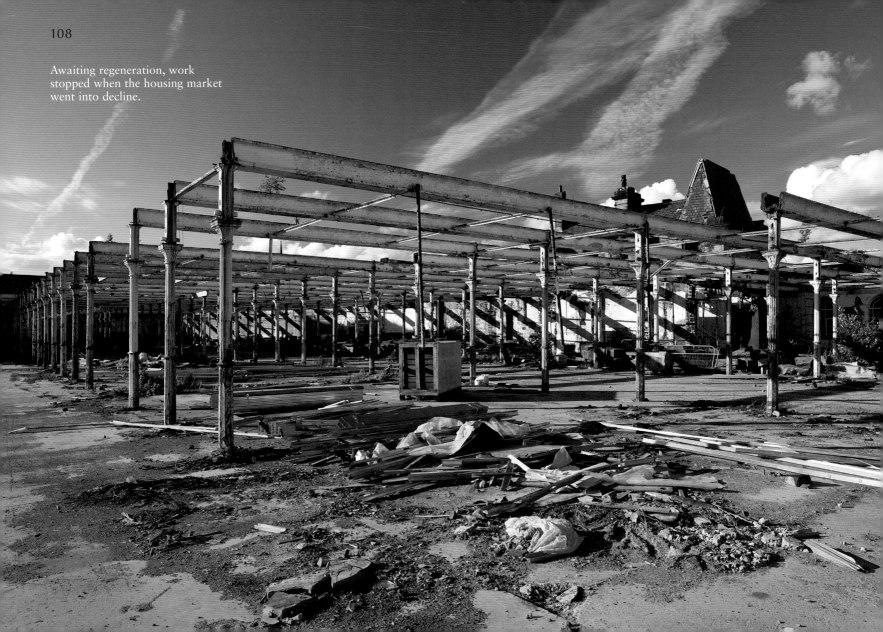

Awaiting regeneration, work
stopped when the housing market
went into decline.

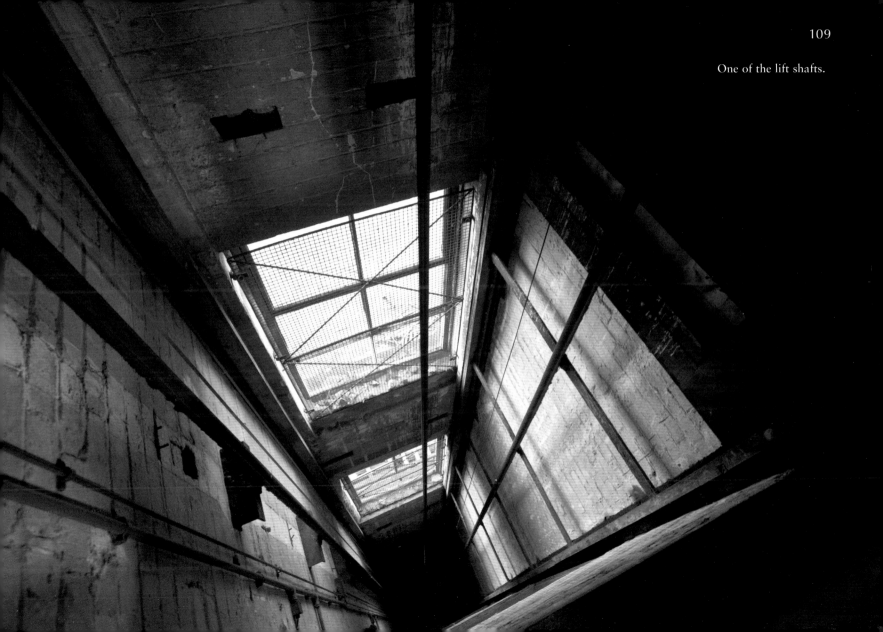

One of the lift shafts.

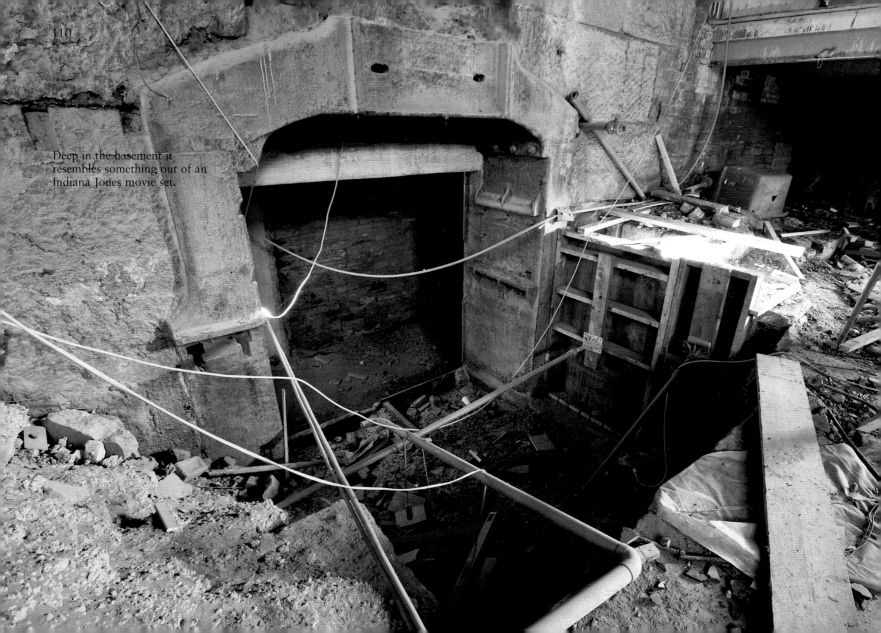

Deep in the basement it resembles something out of an Indiana Jones movie set.

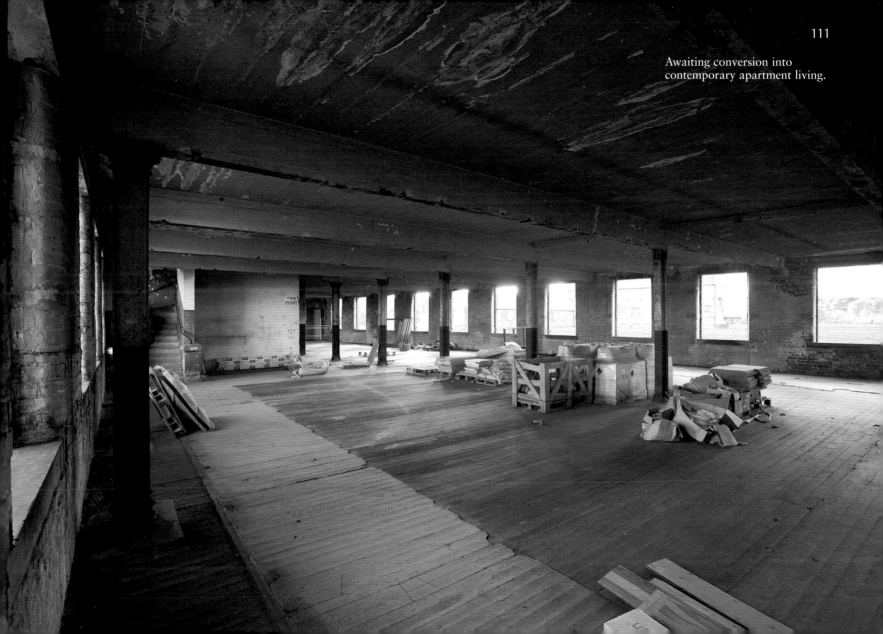

Awaiting conversion into
contemporary apartment living.

WHETLEY MILLS, DANIEL ILLINGWORTH & SONS

Alfred Illingworth (September 1827–1907) was an English worsted spinner and Liberal politician. Alfred was born in Bradford, the son of spinner Daniel Illingworth, who was also of Bradford descent, having been born in 1792 upon the very spot where Messrs D. Illingworth & Sons still stands. Alfred entered the family worsted spinning business at the age of sixteen. In 1865, with his brother Henry, he established Whetley Mills, one of the largest spinning factories in Bradford. He had strong non-conformist and free trade views and ultimately entered into politics. He was elected MP for Knaresborough in 1868, but lost the seat in 1874. He was then elected at Bradford in 1880. In 1885, the constituency was reorganised and he was elected for Bradford West. He lost the seat in 1895. He married Margaret Holden, daughter of Sir Isaac Holden, 1st Baronet, in 1863 and his brother Henry married another daughter of Holden, creating a strong alliance between two of the dominant Bradford families of the time. Henry was the father of Percy Illingworth and Albert Illingworth, who were also active in politics in Yorkshire.

The mill at one time employed over 300 people in the production of worsted yarn. Such was the success of the company that, as late as 1958, they bought Salts Mill in Saltaire for £4.7 million and the entire combing process was transferred from Saltaire to Whetley Mills. In 2014 the old mill is part way through some renovation and restoration.

When Alfred died in 1907, his ashes were placed in a grey granite mausoleum in the style of an Egyptian mastaba, with lotus leaf columns, and sphinxes either side of the doorway at Undercliffe Cemetery. The mausoleum is located just a few feet away from his father's magnificent Egyptian revival tomb.

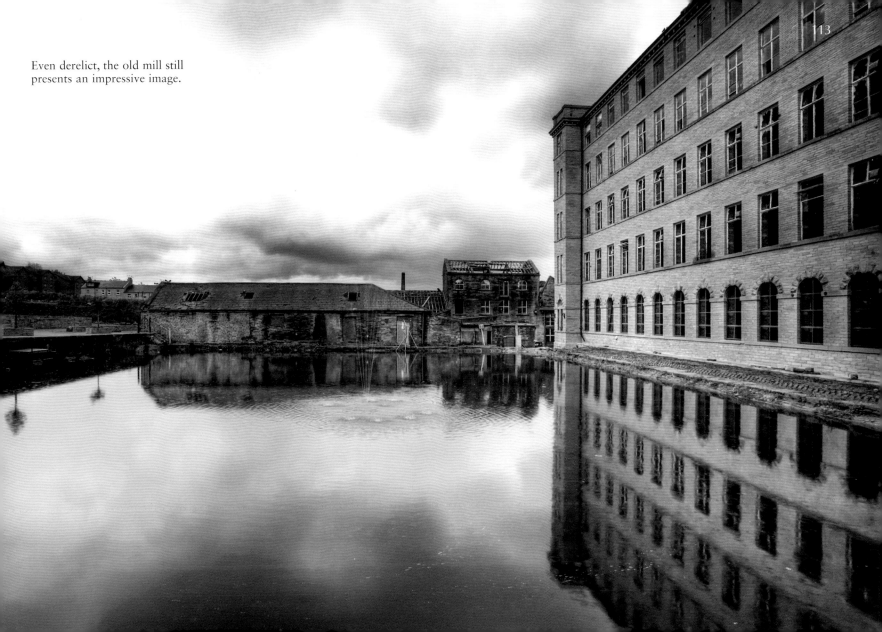

Even derelict, the old mill still presents an impressive image.

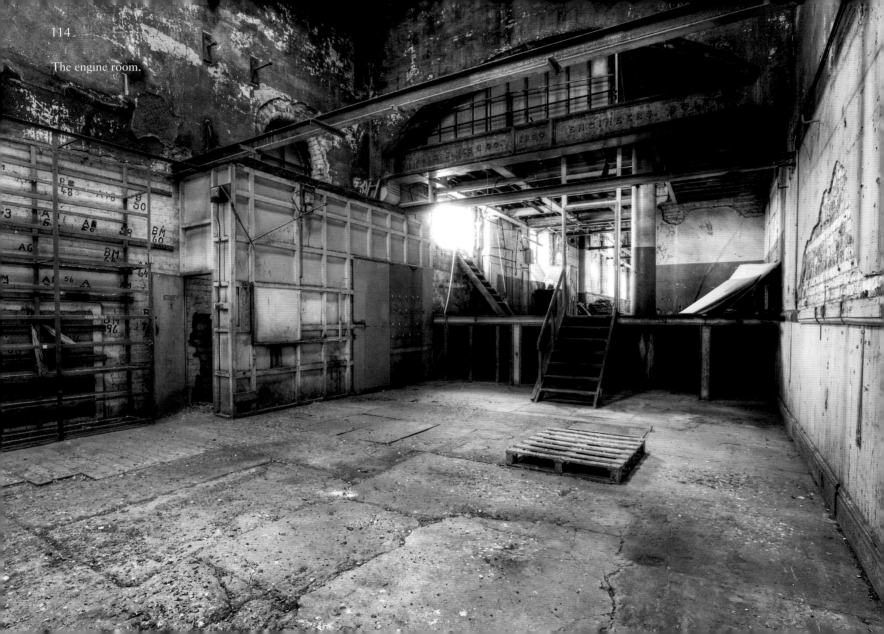

The engine room.

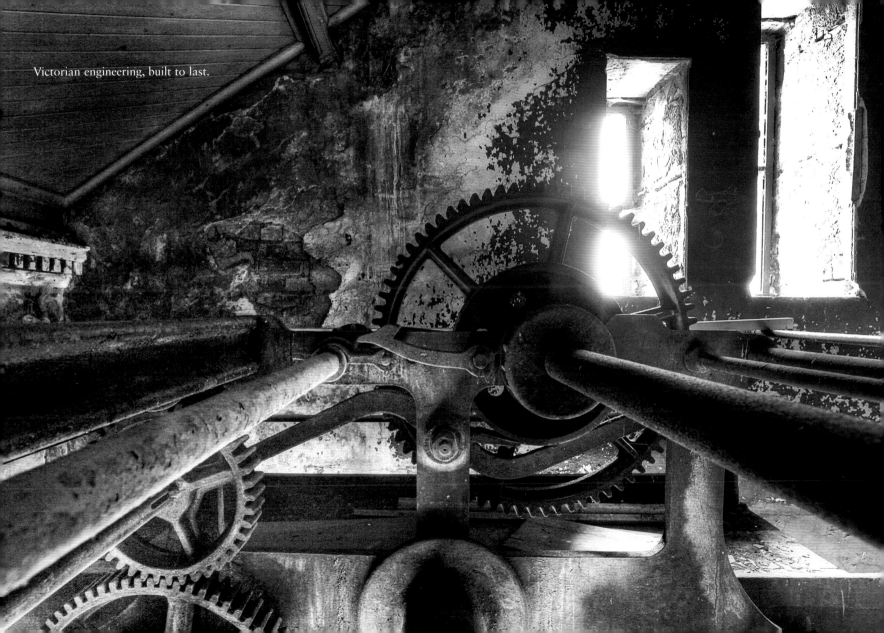

Victorian engineering, built to last.

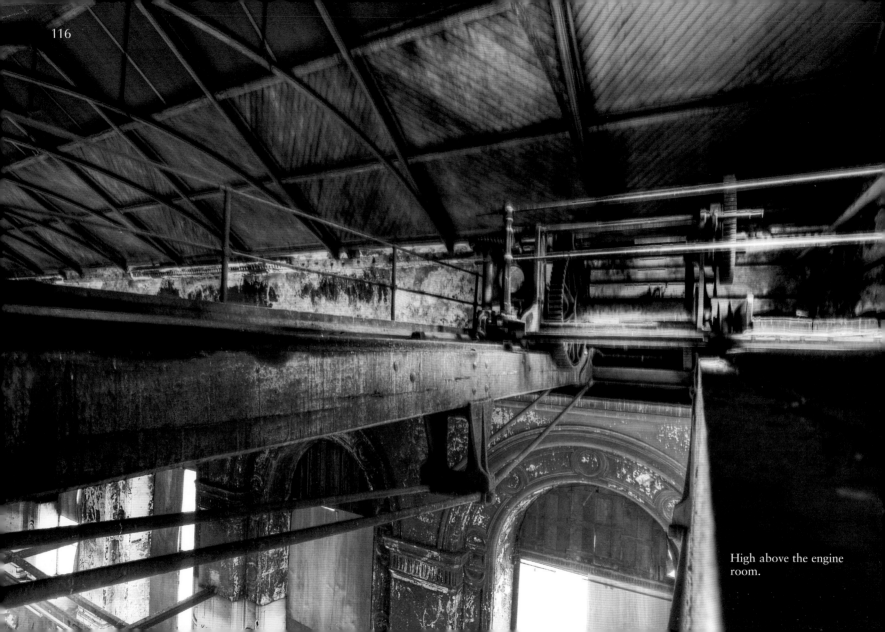

High above the engine room.

THE CHANGING FACE OF BRADFORD

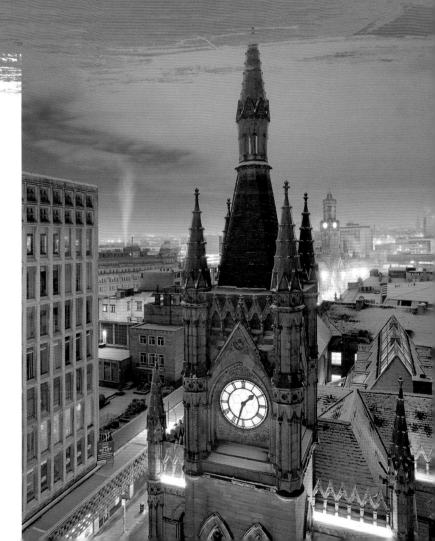

Possibly Samuel Cunliffe Lister, Matthew Thompson, Daniel, and Alfred Illingworth and other notable Bradford worthies might turn in their graves over the decline and loss of so much of Victorian Bradford's rich industrial past; however, they just might approve of recent developments to bring Bradford back from the brink of forever becoming a backwater, in comparison to the wealthier Leeds. During the past few years, massive investments have been made with the new Provident Financial – Jurys Hotel building at Southgate and the fabulous City Park, which is Bradford's brilliant multi-award-winning public space. The Mirror Pool is the largest urban water feature in the UK. The former Forster Square, which was a crater in the centre of Bradford for many years, is at last the subject of a £275-million investment to create the Broadway shopping centre, which will bring big name shopping to the very heart of Bradford. In doing so, there will be 2,500 new retail jobs, which even Prime Minister David Cameron acknowledges as a feather in our cap. Bradford in 2014 comprises of a multicultural society on the edge of becoming a great city again; a city that our forefathers would be proud of. The question is: where has the William Forster statue gone?

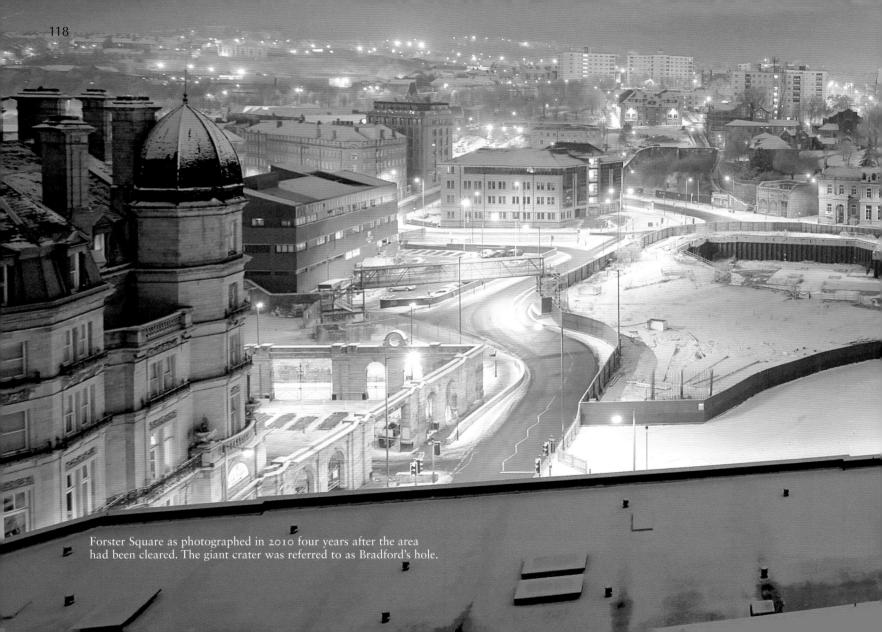

Forster Square as photographed in 2010 four years after the area
had been cleared. The giant crater was referred to as Bradford's hole.

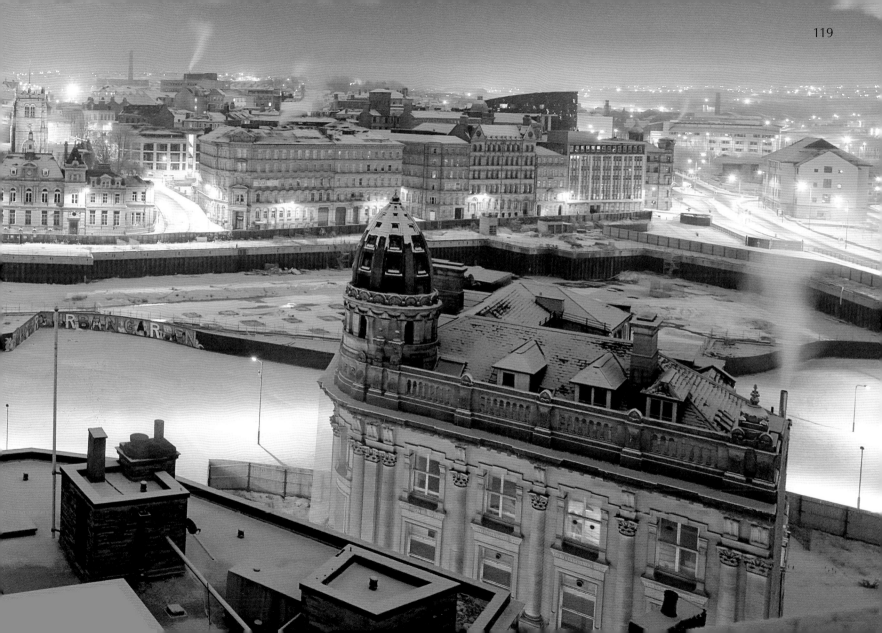

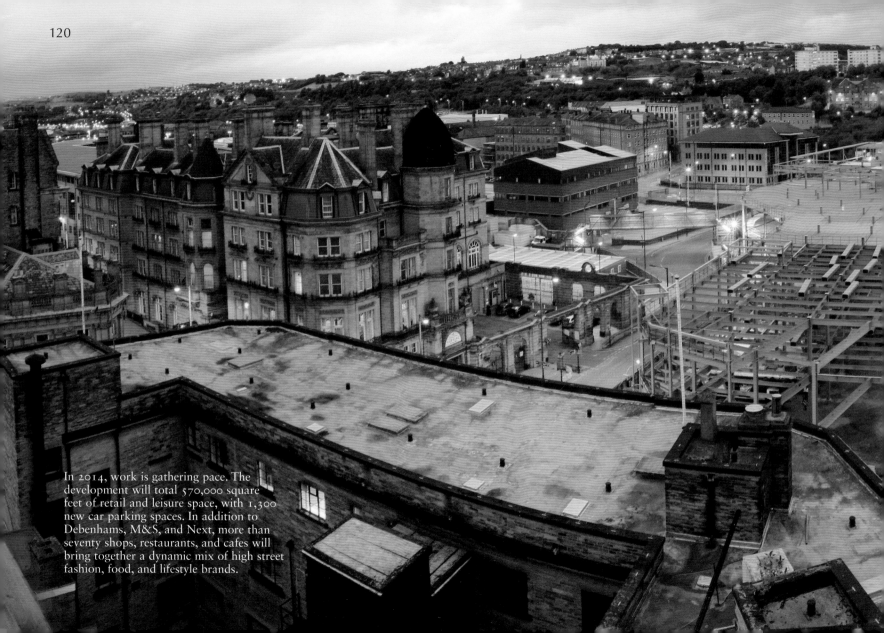

In 2014, work is gathering pace. The development will total 570,000 square feet of retail and leisure space, with 1,300 new car parking spaces. In addition to Debenhams, M&S, and Next, more than seventy shops, restaurants, and cafes will bring together a dynamic mix of high street fashion, food, and lifestyle brands.

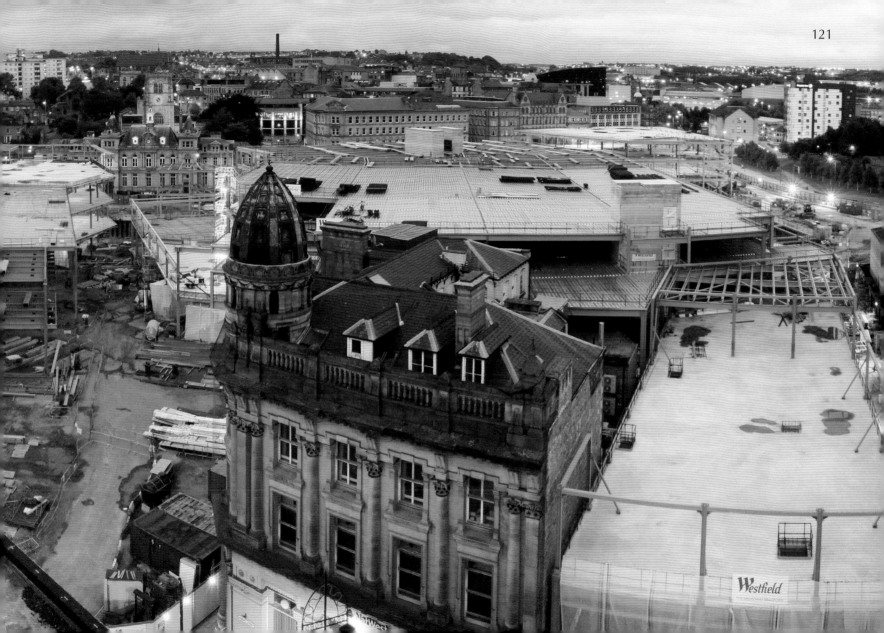

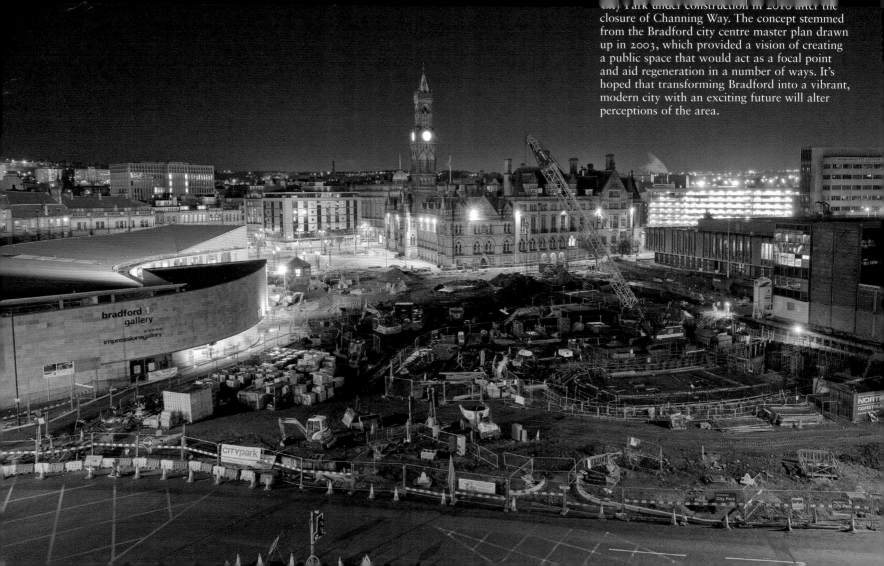

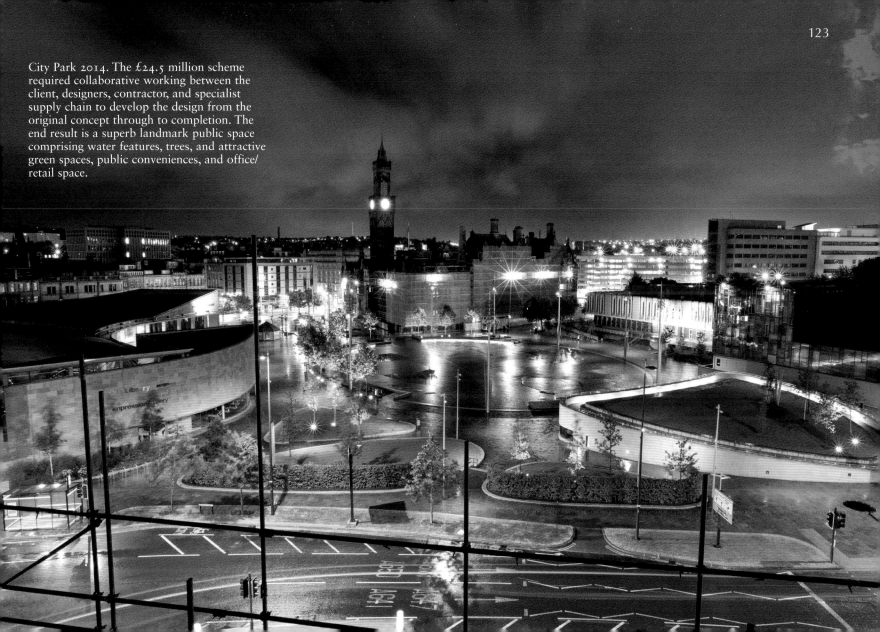

City Park 2014. The £24.5 million scheme required collaborative working between the client, designers, contractor, and specialist supply chain to develop the design from the original concept through to completion. The end result is a superb landmark public space comprising water features, trees, and attractive green spaces, public conveniences, and office/retail space.

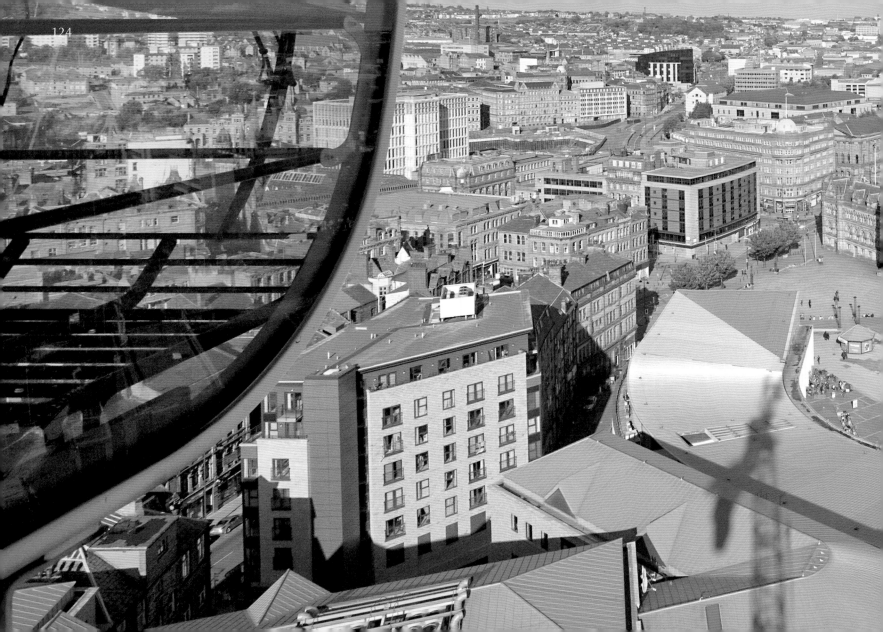

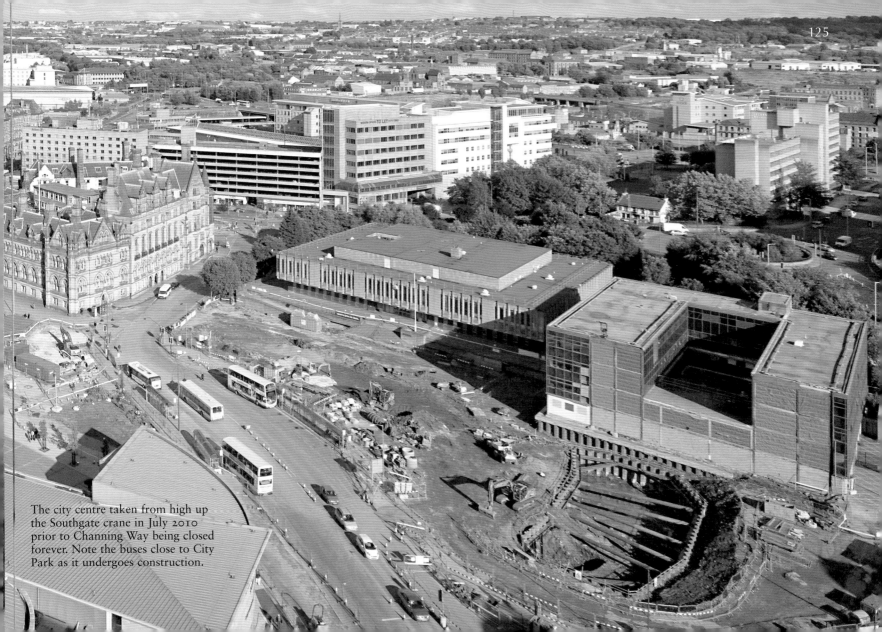

The city centre taken from high up the Southgate crane in July 2010 prior to Channing Way being closed forever. Note the buses close to City Park as it undergoes construction.

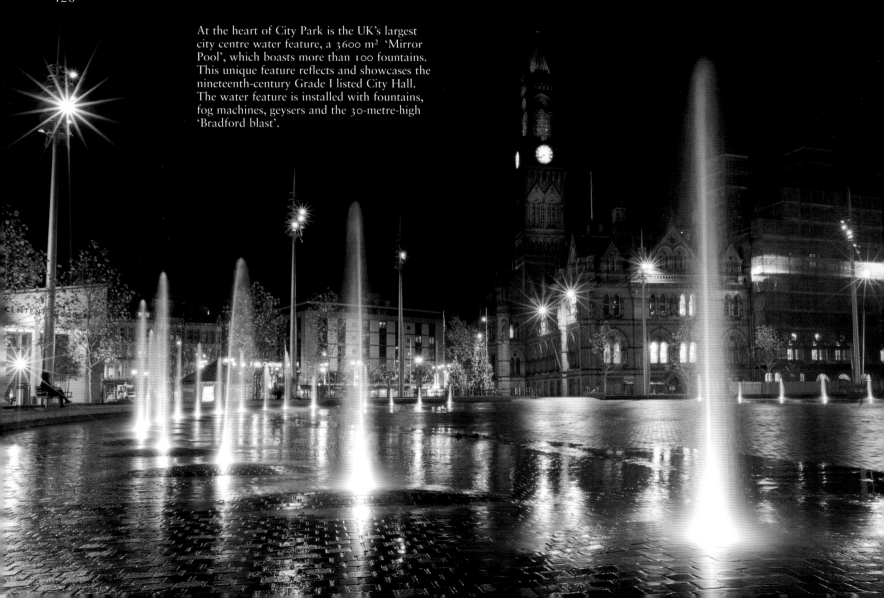

At the heart of City Park is the UK's largest
city centre water feature, a 3600 m² 'Mirror
Pool', which boasts more than 100 fountains.
This unique feature reflects and showcases the
nineteenth-century Grade I listed City Hall.
The water feature is installed with fountains,
fog machines, geysers and the 30-metre-high
'Bradford blast'.

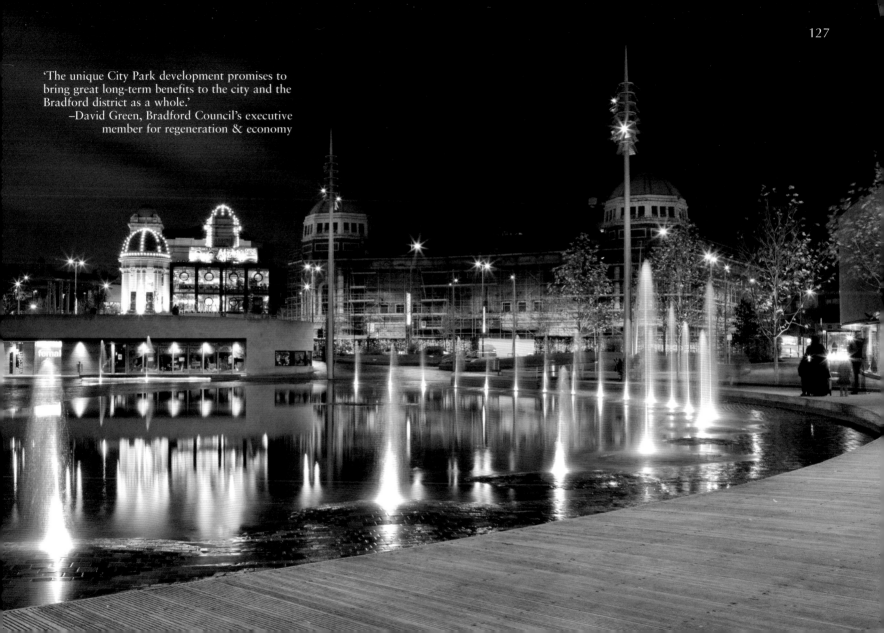

'The unique City Park development promises to bring great long-term benefits to the city and the Bradford district as a whole.'
–David Green, Bradford Council's executive member for regeneration & economy

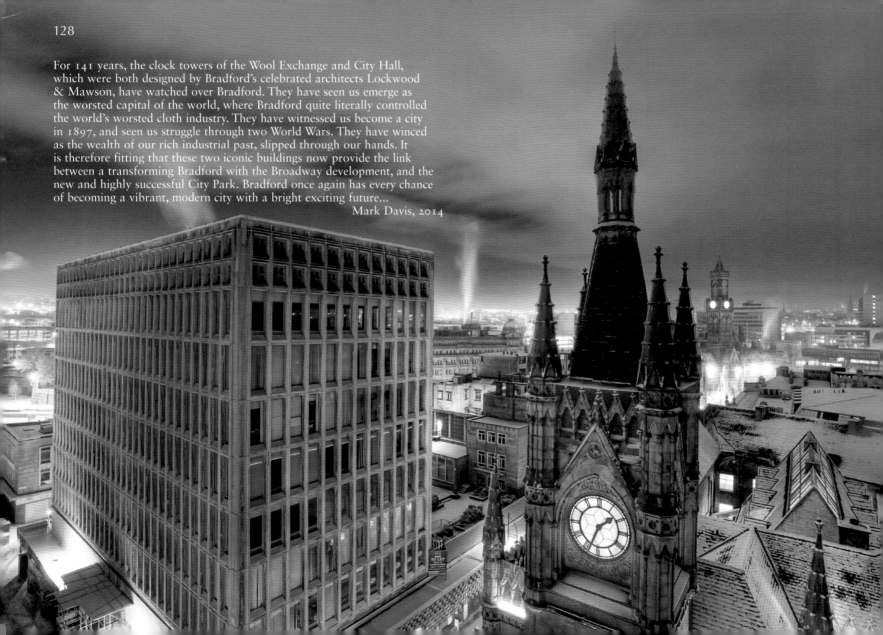

For 141 years, the clock towers of the Wool Exchange and City Hall, which were both designed by Bradford's celebrated architects Lockwood & Mawson, have watched over Bradford. They have seen us emerge as the worsted capital of the world, where Bradford quite literally controlled the world's worsted cloth industry. They have witnessed us become a city in 1897, and seen us struggle through two World Wars. They have winced as the wealth of our rich industrial past, slipped through our hands. It is therefore fitting that these two iconic buildings now provide the link between a transforming Bradford with the Broadway development, and the new and highly successful City Park. Bradford once again has every chance of becoming a vibrant, modern city with a bright exciting future...

Mark Davis, 2014